You Are

Not

Alone

You Are Not Alone

Teens Talk About Life After the Loss of a Parent

LYNNE B. HUGHES

SCHOLASTIC INC.

New York   Toronto   London   Auckland   Sydney
Mexico City   New Delhi   Hong Kong   Buenos Aires

This book is being published simultaneously in hardcover by Scholastic Press.

ISBN: 0-439-58591-0

10 9 8 7 6 5 4 3 2 1   05 06 07 08 09 10

Printed in the United States of America   23

First Scholastic paperback printing, September 2005

The text type was set in Centaur MT

Book design by Elizabeth B. Parisi

To my parents, Marilynn and Skip Barribeau,
and Liz Szabla's dad, Frank Szabla —
their legacy lives on through this book.
And for my children, Evan and Jamie,
and my husband, Kelly.

Acknowledgments

To all the campers who contributed to this project — Greg, Laura, Emily S., Elizabeth, Matt, Amy, Carlos, Peter, Cassie, Lora, Emily L., Mary, Eamon, Franco, Jesse, Brittany, Hilary, Katie, Kimberly, Melly, Caitlin, Tory, Erin, Ella, Casey, Hannah, Emily F., Brianna, Phillip, John, Abby O., and Abbey H. You all hold such a special place in my heart. Thank you for taking the time and the risk of baring your souls to help me create this book. Together we can help more children to heal. You are all amazing!

To the wonderful grief therapists who contributed to this book — Jill FitzGerald, Ed Whitacre, Helen Henrich, Kurt Stiefvater, Kathy O'Keefe: I am so blessed to have had each of you in my "camp life" for many years — and now in my "book life" too. Your input has been invaluable, and I am forever indebted to each of you.

To the CZC parents who nudged their kids to fill out the surveys: God bless you many times over!

To my editor, Liz Szabla, who believed in me and this

book before she even met me. Thanks for finding me and for your faith, passion, and friendship. This book is yours too.

Gary Spector, thank you for letting Liz and me suck you into the world of CZC and for your amazing contributions.

To my supporters at Scholastic, especially Jennifer Rees, Elizabeth Parisi, Karen Nagle, Allison Corbett, and Dave Barrett — you guys ROCK! Thanks for believing in this book and going the extra mile to make it a reality.

To my agent, Elizabeth Kaplan: Thank you for all your behind-the-scenes support.

Heartfelt thanks to Hope Edelman, whose pioneer book *Motherless Daughters* was a catalyst for my founding Comfort Zone Camp, which ultimately led to this book. Thank you for becoming my friend along the way.

Nancy Boyd, you've been my best friend since we were 12: Thanks for being there.

To all the campers who have ever attended Comfort Zone Camp and those who opened their hearts and souls: Your voices are all a part of this book.

To the volunteers, board, and staff of Comfort Zone Camp, who understand the importance of helping to heal grieving children: Your time and energy are what makes it all happen!

Finally, to my husband, Kelly, and my children, Evan and Jamie: Thanks for your support on this important project. I love you all very much.

Contents

Foreword
How I Came to Write This Book

My name is Lynne. My guess is that you and I have something in common. You have lost a parent to death. Me too. I actually had both parents die. My mother died when I was 9 and my father when I was 12. It stinks, doesn't it?

I grew up (and it was hard) and eventually started Comfort Zone Camp, a place for grieving kids who have lost someone they love. Comfort Zone has become the largest grief camp in the country. Thousands of children have attended at no cost. A lot of the kids have returned many times, and I have gotten to know them well. I've heard their stories and watched them grow and heal as they've moved forward on their grief journeys. More than thirty of those kids, all of whom are teens and had a parent die, contributed to this book.

Why am I writing this book? One reason is, as you may have already discovered, there are not many books for kids who have dealt with the death of a parent. There were none when I went through it. I've found that the few books out there tend to be written by people with a lot of credentials after their names, "experts" who want to tell you what *you should do* but haven't necessarily walked the road themselves.

Another reason I'm writing this book is because I never knew if I was going to be okay and I never knew that I wasn't the only one besides my brothers that this had happened to. I want you to know that you are not alone either. One of the best things about Comfort Zone is that almost all the kids who come have never met someone else who has experienced the death of someone close to them. They learn quickly that they are not alone. You may not have had the opportunity to meet another teenager who has experienced the death of a parent either.

Look at the straight line below: It represents you on your journey of grief, pain, hope, and healing.

——————————————————

Right now picture a second line next to yours.

——————————————————

——————————————————

The lines are similar but not exactly the same. They are, however, going in the same direction. That second line is me on my grief journey, now walking beside you.

Now picture thirty other lines next to the first two. These represent all the teens who helped write this book. They too are now walking beside you on your grief journey.

This book is set up in two parts. It starts with my own

personal story, then proceeds to the heart of the book, where teens share their stories, the things they wish they could have known about grief and what they have learned through their losses.

The main thing we want you to know is that you are not alone.

1

Lynne's Story

My life began on April 28, 1964, the day I was born. It began a second time on January 9, 1974. January 9 was the day my mom died. It was a Wednesday morning in the midst of a Michigan winter. Michigan winters are very bleak; the days are mostly gray and foggy, with any hopes for green grass and sunshine a distant memory under the dirty snow.

I woke up that Wednesday morning to the sound of my dad attempting to wake up my mother. He was getting up early to play tennis. My bedroom was right next to theirs. I heard his voice, too loud for that early in the morning, as he said, "Marilynn . . . Mare, honey, wake up. *Wake up!*"

I stumbled out of bed into the dark doorway. I asked my dad what was wrong. He told me to turn on the light. I did and was blinded, as if a camera flash had gone off in my eyes. As I stood there, shielding my eyes from the harsh light, my father stammered in frantic disbelief, "I think your mother is dead." I screamed and ran into the room my three brothers shared and screamed, "Wake up! Mom is dead!" I ran downstairs to find my grandmother — my mother's mother — who lived with us. "Wake up, Mom is dead!" I screamed again. She and I ran back upstairs into my parents' bedroom. We saw my dad and my brothers, Danny and Matt, sitting on the bed, while my oldest brother, Marc, who was then 14, attempted to give Mom CPR.

What happened next was a blur. A neighbor was called and asked to watch two of my brothers and me, and we were quickly whisked away. As we walked down the driveway, we were met by the ambulance that had come to take my mother. We were also greeted by the gray, foggy, gloomy day that would be the backdrop for most of my memories over the next couple of years. I remember thinking over and over again that what was happening was a bad dream and that I just needed to wake up.

I went from the first neighbor's house to the next without going home. My brothers went to another neighbor's house. I did not speak with my father during that time. Two nights later, I somehow wound up at the funeral home. I still didn't know how my mother had died. I still didn't believe she was gone.

My mother was the glue that bonded my whole family. She made us click. That first week, and for a very long time after, I missed her presence from the moment I woke up until the time I went to bed. At times I would avoid the things that reminded me of her, and at other times I would find myself going into her room, touching things in her jewelry box or smelling pieces of clothing to try to feel close to her.

It was a Catholic funeral, so there were two days of viewing followed by the funeral the next morning. The worst part was the viewing. It was bizarre to see a dead person for the first time. It was bizarre that the person was my mother. The makeup was gross, and the embalming fluid made her skin and fingernails look funny. I remember overhearing someone say that she never would have wanted to be buried in the dress she was in. It wasn't her color, this person said; who had picked it out? I didn't know.

My mother had the largest viewing the funeral home had ever held. There were so many people there. The air was thick and heavy and the smell of flowers was overwhelming. My cousin Mike, who was also 9, fainted during the wake. To this day, a strong whiff of a flower arrangement instantly takes me back to my mother's funeral and the funeral home.

On the way to the funeral, I rode in a limo for the first time and remember thinking it was cool but that I really shouldn't be enjoying it too much. Afterward, everyone came back to our house. I enjoyed seeing all my relatives and playing with my cousins. I remember thinking it was weird to be having so much fun. I remember two of my uncles having too much to drink and having to be separated before they punched each other on our porch. I remember our neighbor

Mrs. Brady telling me she would come and visit me every day after school to see how I was doing. I was so touched. She really seemed to care. I felt like someone would be looking out for me.

And I overheard how my mother had died: A blood clot had traveled through my mother's lungs, causing one of them to collapse. The visualization of her lung collapsing scared me almost as much as knowing she was gone.

What I know now and didn't understand then is that you cry at a funeral because you've lost someone very important to you, but it is not until you live every day afterward that you realize exactly what you have lost. I didn't understand then that I was crying at my mother's funeral for all the hurt and loss that was going to be. When the funeral ended and the food was finished and all the relatives and friends left our house to get back to their own lives, my long grief journey began. I would never be the person I was before that first of many gloomy, gray days.

My neighbor never came by after school. I was very hurt. It was the first time an adult had not come through with a promise to me. I never really trusted her again, and for a long time after that, I had a hard time trusting people in general.

At my father's request, my grandma, who had lived with us since I was two months old, moved out within a week of my mother's death. My grandparents from Arizona — my father's parents — whom my father was not very close to, moved in to take care of us. My brother Marc had been in a lot of trouble before Mom died; he was supposed to have gone to military school but didn't because my father felt sorry for him. After a few days off from school, my other brothers and I were expected to get back to our routine of school and homework, although nothing about our routine was the same. My dad rarely came home and often stayed out late drinking. He slept on the couch because he didn't want to sleep in the empty bed my mother had died in. We stopped going to church because my dad (who was a devout Catholic and had considered becoming a priest) was angry at God. At some point several months later, my dad's sister and her daughters packed up my mother's things.

No one ever talked about my mother or the pain we were all in. We were expected to act as if her death had never happened. In a sense, we were expected to act as if she had never lived.

My grief came out sideways and front ways and mostly in quiet ways. I remember just trying to make it through each day and adapt to all the changes and chaos that were going on in my house. I tried not to think about my mom — it wasn't a safe thing to do in my survival mode. I remember my mom's mom being so fearful of me forgetting my mother that she would say things to me like, "Your mom would have wanted you to do this" or "Your mom wouldn't have wanted you to do that." Or "You remember _____ about your mom, don't you?" After a while, I would tell her no, I didn't remember _____ even when I did, because I didn't want to talk about it.

I was afraid to go to sleep because I was afraid someone would die during the night. I insisted on a night light. Somehow if the light was on and I woke up and could see, then everything was okay. I started to believe that people could only die if it was dark. When I woke up in the middle of the night (which was frequently), the first thing I would do was put my hand on my heart to make sure it was beating and make sure I could swallow, which in my mind meant that my lung had not collapsed. Even today, thirty years later, when I wake up in the middle of the night, I still catch myself checking for my heartbeat and seeing if I can swallow.

When I thought about my mother and the mental picture of her dying, I would be hit with a sudden tightness in my throat and the overwhelming fear of not being able to swallow. The more I would think about it, the tighter my throat would get; I'd run and get a glass of water, thinking over and over that if I could swallow, my lungs hadn't collapsed and I wasn't dying.

Although I didn't know it then, these episodes were panic attacks. One night when my glass of water didn't calm me down, I shared with someone for the first time that I had a lump in my throat and felt like I couldn't swallow or breathe. My dad called the pediatrician, who made a house call. The doctor told me I was okay. But I didn't feel okay.

The next day, my grandfather took me to the pediatrician's office. The doctor proceeded to roll out an anatomy chart and deliver a very sterile, technical explantion of the mechanics of swallowing. The message was nothing is wrong with you. I felt like a complete idiot, like I was making the whole thing up. My grandfather acted as if this explanation should put an end to the whole thing. It's amazing to me that no one dared acknowledge the obvious: I was a scared little girl who was grieving for her mother. No one gave me what I really needed: a big hug and the reassurance that I would be okay.

I want to say here that my father was one of the most charismatic and fun people you could ever meet. I was crazy about him. He made me feel like a princess in his presence and he loved us all very much. That being said, he struggled horribly and was lost in his own grief after my mom died. I don't love him any less as a result; he just didn't set the best example of what "to do" after a death in the family.

He stayed out most of the time. He went to work and didn't come home till very late. What I didn't understand then was that he couldn't cope with his own grief, let alone that of his four children. He added a new layer of chaos to our lives when he started dating a couple of months after my mom's death. Interestingly, the first woman he dated was my mom's hairdresser, who a lot of people thought resembled my mother. I had always liked her, and I still liked her, but I couldn't understand why my dad would date her and she'd date my dad. She was the first of many, many dates my father would bring around. Some of them were nice; some not so nice.

My father eventually put an addition on our house — a new master bedroom. He began to come home a little more and sleep in the new room. On many of the nights I couldn't sleep, I went into the new room to sleep in the bed with him. We never talked about that.

My Arizona grandparents, who were not particularly warm and fuzzy people, were responsible for hiring a series of live-in housekeepers. Shortly after they hired someone, my father would fly them back to Arizona. When a housekeeper didn't work out (which was usually shortly thereafter), my father would fly my grandparents back and let them take care of firing and rehiring. Over the next year, we went through more than four housekeepers, ranging from pretty incompetent to pretty interesting. One even taught us karate — she lasted six months.

A year after my mother died, my father began dating a woman he married three months later. My dad and she had a meeting with us to tell us they were engaged. My older brother Marc said she was marrying my dad for his money and stormed out of the house. Danny, Matt, and I started crying and said we thought it was too soon after Mom died and that we didn't want a new mother. When Jean, my stepmother-to-be, started to cry, I felt a bit sorry for her, but I still didn't want them to get married.

As soon as they returned home from their honeymoon, my grandparents pulled us kids aside and bluntly told us, "She is your mom now, and you will call her Mom." I didn't like it and protested, but in a way, it did make me feel more like all the other kids I knew to have someone to call Mom. I did as I was told.

Jean had three kids of her own — two daughters who were in college and a 16-year-old son. (I found out later that she had been married three times before she married my father.) The blended-family thing did not go well in my house. There were some violent fights involving my brother Marc and my new stepbrother, who were both into alcohol and drugs, with my dad taking Marc's side and Jean taking her son's side.

About a year into their marriage, my father left Jean and left us with her. He said he'd made a big mistake and lived somewhere else for about a month. At one point he came home to get more clothes, and I told him he was an ass for leaving. Even though I was only 12, I felt he was entitled to my opinion. He made me buy into this whole stepmother-blended-family thing, I went along with it, and then when he'd decided he'd made a mistake, he was the only one to leave?

My father came back just as suddenly as he had left. He quit drinking, went to Alcoholics Anonymous meetings, and lost weight. He started playing the best golf and tennis of his life and even came home more. Things seemed better.

One Sunday, my dad and Jean were playing golf, and my brothers and I were following them around when Jean and my father had a tiff. The golf game ended, and my brothers rode home with my stepmother while I rode home with my dad. All of a sudden, my dad blurted out to me, "I never should have married Jean. I never loved her. I still love your mother!"

Just when things seemed better, this revelation was very uncomfortable, to say the least. I had been clinging to our fragile home life, and now it seemed it might crash down again. I said, "Dad, don't tell me that!" He replied, "I'm sorry, but it's true." The conversation ended.

A few weeks later that same summer, I woke up to my step-brother telling me that my father had chest pains and had been taken to the hospital. It turned out that my father had had a massive heart attack. He was only 45 years old. He was put on a ventilator. For three weeks, I stayed at my aunt's house while my father was transferred to a different hospital with a better cardiac unit. I wasn't allowed to visit him. I saw my stepmother one time at a social function. Someone asked her how my dad was, and I saw her give them the "thumbs down." I realized then, for the first time, that my dad might die too.

My dad had open-heart surgery. I was with my brothers at an aunt's house during the surgery. I remember the phone call coming during an episode of *The $20,000 Pyramid*. My cousin came in and told us my dad hadn't made it.

My life began a third time on September 7, 1976. I was 12.

I didn't want to go to my father's funeral. I'd been through it before. It wasn't that I had any doubt he had died; I just dreaded the journey I was about to begin.

I learned almost immediately that there is no right or wrong way to handle grief — just a lot of *different* ways. My dad died the day before I was to begin seventh grade and junior high. Starting seventh grade was a big deal in my life, and I decided to go to school that first day. It was only a half day and I wanted to be like everyone else — not showing up would tag me as different from day one. But it was one of the hardest days of my life.

I knew junior high meant six classes with six different teachers plus homeroom. All we did that first half day was go to each of these classes and meet the teachers. In each of these seven classes, each teacher read their attendance roster and verified your name, parents' names, address, and phone number. I sat there each time — gulping for air — as I confirmed my father's name, biting back the words that he just died yesterday. It was horrible. I walked home in a daze. To make matters worse, my brother Matt met me on the driveway and told me that I was a terrible person for going to school and that my stepmother thought I was too. He said that if I'd really loved our dad, I would not have gone to school that day. I told him that everyone grieves differently and just because I went to school, it did not mean that I didn't love him.

After my dad died, I felt like a picture window that had been completely shattered. I knew I had to somehow put all the pieces back together, but I wasn't sure how. Sympathetic adults marveled at my ability to "cope." To me, it was never a choice. I knew that if I laid down, no one was going to pick me up. I had two choices: either to stay on the ground or to pick myself up.

I eventually discovered that my father had made my stepmother our legal guardian. However, he had not changed his will — everything was still left to my mother. This began a series of emotional and, ultimately, legal battles with my stepmother that shaped and reshaped my relationship with her. The details of our legal battles focused mostly on money, and I felt as if I "owed" my stepmother and that I needed to be extra good, not only to try to get her to love me but also to try to make up for this "injustice" my father had caused.

The one thing that my brothers and I clung to was staying in the same house, so we could go to the same schools and have the same friends. My brother Marc hated my stepmother and dropped out of school the spring after my dad died and moved out of the house. I have barely seen him since. He was going down a dark path before my parents died and spiraled down farther afterward.

Matt and my youngest brother, Danny, were totally immersed in their friends. Danny, who was 6 when my mom died and 9 when my father died, became afraid of his own shadow.

My stepmother would tell us periodically that she could "leave any time" and that she was "doing us a favor by raising us." This scared all of us, Danny in particular. Somehow I became the "safe" person for him to go to, and I fell into the role of surrogate mom. And even though I was younger than Matt, I fell into the same role with him. It wasn't because I was extra nice or nurturing. It was because I was the one who was there the most and was female. We knew even at that age that we should be checking in with someone and asking if we could go places. I became the one who knew where everyone was, and in Danny's case, the one to tell him to come home.

I longed for my stepmother to love me and tried to paint

myself whatever color she might like — even if that meant being purple one day and becoming yellow the next. The spring after my dad died, I remember dropping hints to try to get her to say she loved me, but she told me that she would never love me the same as she did her own three children, nor should I expect her to. She explained that this wasn't something I would understand until I had children of my own. I was devastated. I tried to be strong and rationalize what she was saying to understand her position. Another part of me felt the few pieces I had put back in the picture window break all over again.

I dealt with the aftermath of my parents' deaths by keeping most of my feelings to myself. I cried a lot in private, in my room. I was lucky to have one very close friend, Nancy, who I could share almost everything with. I also kept a journal and wrote a lot of poems. My goal became getting through each day without crying. I didn't necessarily aim to be happy, I just didn't want to cry. I had once had dreams of being a famous person or an actress, but at that point all I wished for was just to be okay. I didn't feel comfortable with other kids my age. I felt like I was dealing with the United Nations, and they were dealing with their goldfish dying. I longed to put the United Nations away and be carefree like everyone else. I rarely did sleepovers unless it was with Nancy. I just couldn't put my serious side away to be fun and silly like other girls my age.

On the outside I continued to excel in school and extra-curricular activities: I was president of the student council and captain of the cheerleading squad, and I enjoyed playing sports. But on the inside I struggled with everything I did. Things I knew I could do became such a challenge. I longed for the confident, secure person I felt I was before my parents' deaths and tried to push away my feelings of fear and insecurity. Most days, I was unsure of which Lynne was going to show up for any given task, whether it was raising my hand in class to answer a question or being able to participate in sporting or social events. I sometimes felt as if I were going crazy. Mostly, I wondered if I could ever rebuild myself to be the person who I was meant to be before losing my parents.

My stepmother had legal battles with my father's estate the whole time I lived with her. It escalated during my junior year of high school into court appearances for me and my brothers, where we testified how we wanted her to have whatever money she needed so that we could stay together and not have to move, lose our friends, and go to new schools.

At the same time, four girls at school decided they hated me. I never knew exactly what I'd done — in fact, the one who hated me the most I had never even met. They yelled mean things at me when I walked down the hall, they elbowed me into lockers, and they threatened to beat me up. I had to get people to walk with me in the halls to classes. I wanted to be liked — *needed* to be liked — and school had been a place where I could at least go through the motions of being "normal." And then these girls made school miserable for me. That, along with the situation at home, brought on crippling stress headaches. One of my teachers would let me go home early so I could rest. I confided in a teacher and my guidance counselor how unhappy I was. At home, I spent a lot of time in my room, crying and missing my parents more than I could say.

After the judge turned down my stepmother's request for more money, I believed I now had to go live with relatives. I asked my aunt if I could live with her. At this point I had decided it would be a relief to get away from my stepmother and the girls who hated me at school — even if it meant not living with my brothers and leaving my friends. My stepmother was furious and told me that my parents would be spitting on me from heaven and rolling over in their graves. My aunt came and got me the next morning.

This all happened in March of my junior year. Matt went on to graduate from high school that June. He moved out that summer. My stepmother decided to let Danny move in with some neighbors down the street who offered guardianship. I did not speak to her until three months after I'd moved in with my aunt, at my brother's graduation. It was awkward, but she was friendly. At one point she and I wound up in the kitchen together, and she said, "I want you to know that even though I never said it, I always loved you." To this day I'm still trying to make sense of it all.

I wish I could tell you that things started to look up when I moved in with my aunt, who was my father's sister. She was a lot of fun, and you could swear in front of her, which at 16, I thought was cool. My uncle, however, wasn't known for being very friendly. Still, I thought, how bad could he be? My aunt was great, and I bet that if my uncle got to know me, he would love me.

I was wrong.

It turned out my uncle hadn't wanted me to move in with them, but my aunt had overruled him. His first words to me were, "I'll never love you as a father or an uncle, nor should you expect me to." My heart sank hard. I realized I had escaped one bad situation and put myself right back in another.

The fall of my senior year, I found out I had to graduate early to continue to get social security benefits through college. Luckily, I had enough credits to graduate early and get into a community college. I attended classes and worked after school at a local racquetball club. My new independence meant that I spent more hours away from home and my uncle, which was a big relief.

I went through commencement ceremonies in June with a

graduating class I had not spent even a full year with. I started college at Michigan State that fall and never spent another night in my uncle's house.

When I share my story, many people inevitably ask me how I survived the loss of my parents and all the chaos that accompanied these losses. Even as I write this, I can't believe all of this happened to me. But there are people who also hear my story and understand that these difficult losses are sometimes a part of life. Perhaps someone has gone through similar experiences; perhaps theirs have been much, much worse than mine. What I have learned is that one of the best ways to begin letting go of the pain caused by grief is by sharing our stories. I am a big believer in the concept that every time you tell your story, you heal a little bit. And every time you hear someone else's story, you heal some more.

It helped me to talk with my best and most trusted friend, Nancy. And writing helped too — I kept journals for years. I gave myself pep talks in my journals and began to believe that the worst that could happen to me had already happened and that better things were ahead of me: love, happiness, doing something meaningful with my life.

Counseling also helped. While I wish I had had counseling when I was younger, I'm grateful for the two therapists I saw in my late twenties and early thirties, who helped me find so much of what had been missing from my healing through their listening, guidance, and encouragement. In many ways, they were my "paid parents."

During college, I'd worked as a camp counselor and loved the summer camp life. It was at camp that I met another counselor, Kelly, who I later married. In 1995, I became involved with Motherless Daughters, an organization based on the best-selling book of the same name. Later, Kelly and I were both working at different jobs when he asked, "Are we ever going to get back into camping?" I said yes — and I knew I wanted our camp to be a grief camp for kids. I wanted to catch kids during the grief process and let them meet others who had experienced a significant death, and see firsthand that they weren't alone. I wanted them to be around people who were comfortable talking about death and grief and remembering lost loved ones. I wanted to create an environment I hadn't found — but had certainly longed for — after the deaths of my parents.

You may not know or have had the opportunity to meet another teen who has suffered the death of a parent. Most Comfort Zone campers have never met another person who has lost a parent until they arrive at camp. As a result of coming to camp, they now know that they are not alone. We want you to know that you are not alone too.

It's why I'm sharing my story, and why the teens who I interviewed for this book are sharing their thoughts and feelings about their losses. We know each loss is different and unique. However, although each loss is different, there are still a lot of threads that connect us. I hope that as you read this, you will feel like you're finding a family that you belong to but never knew you had. A family that "gets it."

All of the teens who contributed to this book have been to Comfort Zone Camp at least one time. They were asked questions based on common issues that are most often raised at camp, and their responses appear here in their own words. I also drew from my own experiences and perspective on the loss of a parent.

In this book we talk about what happens after the funeral, after all the relatives have gone home, the casseroles delivered by neighbors have been eaten, and routines such as school, work, and sports are expected to go back to "normal." We talk about how it feels when you start to figure out how your life has changed and what exactly it is that you have lost. Sadly, no one gives out a "how to" manual; it's all new and scary and often lonely.

In this book, you'll also hear from some of our Healing Circle leaders. Healing Circle leaders are grief therapists who volunteer at camp and lead small groups called Healing Circles^{SM} in which we share our memories of our loved ones, our fears, and our sadness. In a Healing Circle, one camper can hear another say, "I feel the same way" or "I went through that too." This book also includes coping strategies and ideas to help you stay connected to your loved one.

I know that healing after the loss of a parent can be a tough journey. Moving forward may take asking for help, asking for answers, and opening up to the people in your life. You may have to ask more than one person to get the help or answers you need. Keep asking. Keep talking. Not doing so can lead to a lot of complications in your life, both now and as you get older.

Take the risk of reading this book. Keep turning the pages. Each page you turn represents a step forward in your healing. Maybe when you finish, you'll feel as if you've run a marathon. The good news is that you'll know you can complete that marathon and survive . . . maybe even with a smile on your face.

2

GRIEF STINKS

*The hardest thing about my loss it that
it will never go away.*

Before we go any farther, I want to put something on the table that needs to be said: Grief stinks! It's unfair, it's something you had no control over, and it's something that you should not have to deal with as a kid. I know lots of teens who feel cheated or ripped off when comparing themselves to other kids or realizing everything they didn't get to do with their loved one and all the memories they won't have together.

We asked the teens who helped with this book what stinks the most. We also asked them to describe the hardest thing about their losses. You'll see a lot of common themes and probably some things you can relate to. You might even have some new things to add to the list.

What would you say is the hardest thing about your loss? What would you say stinks the most? The answers you give are likely to change over time. When teens discuss the most difficult things about their losses at camp in our Healing Circles, it's often the first time many of them realize that they're not alone in what they miss about their parent or the challenges they now face but never bargained for.

Many teens agree that the hardest thing is the empty space no one else can fill. Seventeen-year-old Cassie lost her father when she was 15. He was the manager of a movie theater and was at work when he suffered a massive heart attack. Cassie and her mother both worked at the theater, and both were there when Cassie's father died. She describes facing this reality as she reflects on growing up without her father:

> When I lost my dad, I lost a part of my life. I lost my father figure forever, my hero. He would no longer be there to encourage me. He would no longer be there to dance in the living room with me. He would never teach me how to drive. He would never dance with me on my wedding day or walk me down the aisle. I would never be able to hear his voice again, or listen to his laugh. I would have no one to share the song "Butterfly Kisses" with anymore. People get that losing a parent is hard, but I don't think they fully understand everything we lose with them. It isn't just a person that is lost, it is a lifetime worth of memories yet to be made.

Many of the teens I surveyed, like Cassie, mourn the idea of the future they won't have with their parents. Seventeen-year-old Matt, whose mother died suddenly of a brain aneurysm just as he was about to begin high school, describes just a handful of the big and small milestones, the everyday routines that make losing his mother all the more painful:

> *The hardest thing is my mom not being there for high*
> *school, graduation, homecoming, prom, college, and just not*
> *having that presence of a mom. Everyone loves Mom. She's*
> *your mom, and she always knows the right things to say.*
> *She was always home when I got home from school, and I*
> *hate it that my sister has to come home to an empty house.*
> *I always loved coming home to see her and telling her*
> *about my day — whether it was a good day or a bad*
> *day, it was great to tell her.*

There is also the pressure to "fill their shoes," especially if you've lost a parent of the same sex or if you are the oldest. Eighteen-year-old Abbey H. was 14 when her mother died of a stroke:

> *The hardest things for me were the age I was; the need for*
> *maternal comfort and advice; the distant relationship*
> *with the surviving parent; my mom not being there for*
> *the big moments in my life; tension between my mother's*
> *and father's families; responsibility of feeling like I had*
> *to fill her shoes.*

Sixteen-year-old Melissa was 12 when her mother died of a drug overdose. She expresses what so many teens have shared at CZC about how difficult it is to face the reality of their losses:

The hardest thing is knowing that my mom is really dead and that she is never coming back. This is what really hurts. Sometimes I have nightmares and flashbacks about my mom, and when I do, it feels like the rest of my past is coming back, and then the grieving process starts all over again. Also knowing that the rest of my life when I need her most she won't be here. I want to talk to her and I can't. I want to sit in her lap and cry when I need to. I want to come home from school and tell her about my day, but it is never going to happen. That is what really hurts the most.

For Melissa, these feelings are part of what isolates her from her peers. But she is not alone in missing the security and comfort of her mother's presence. Fifteen-year-old Hilary's father died in the 9/11 attack on the World Trade Center. Here she describes some of the things that are difficult about her loss:

Everything is hard in the beginning, even brushing your teeth or doing your homework. It is still really hard when

my dad doesn't just come walking through that door and
shout, "I'm home," like I am half expecting him to. It's hard
to watch my mom cry. It's hard to deal with that lonely
feeling in the pit of your stomach or the empty feeling in
the house that used to be filled to the brim with laughter.

Fourteen-year-old Eamon's father also died on 9/11. He and his family had to also focus on practical matters:

The hardest thing about my loss is that it was so sudden
and there were all these legal issues my family had to
deal with.

When you've lost a parent, there are things that are hard, and then there are things that just stink. Sixteen-year-old Hannah's father died when she was 9. She describes a longing for everyday rituals that many teens echo:

The thing that stinks the most about my loss is to walk
down the street and see a father and his daughter holding
hands or playing and me thinking that I will never again
have those times with my father. Another thing is that I
now dread my wedding day because I know that I will not
have my father there to walk me down the aisle and give
me away. Lastly, I won't have my father at home to scare

the boys I am dating. I know that most girls would give
anything for their fathers not to grill their boyfriends, but
it is something I have never experienced and never will.

Eighteen-year-old Elizabeth was 12 when her father died suddenly of a heart attack while he was jogging. She also finds it painful to witness father-daughter moments, which make her reflect on all she's missing out on:

It's hard seeing dads and daughters having a great time
together. If I see a little girl with her dad, it makes me sad
not only that I don't have my dad, but that maybe that
little girl doesn't realize how lucky she is that she has hers.
I know it's hard to appreciate someone that much and
think with that mind-set until they're gone, but I just
wish that everyone who has people in their lives would just
realize that any day they could be gone. It stinks that I
didn't know how much my dad meant to me until he died.

The majority of the daughters I've met at camp share Hannah and Elizabeth's feelings about what they are missing out on by not having their fathers in their lives, especially for traditional rites of passage such as weddings. But 16-year-old Emily S., Elizabeth's younger sister, offers another perspective:

For a tomboy like me, losing a dad was hard. He had
been my soccer coach and taught me to play football and
softball.

Emily L., who was 15 when her father died from brain cancer, mourns father-daughter moments too, but also deals with changes in her family life and structure:

> *I felt like I had to grow up really fast. My mom had a*
> *difficult time coping with the loss of my father, and I often*
> *felt and still sometimes feel like I'm the parent and*
> *she's the kid. Don't get me wrong, she's a wonderful mom.*
> *I just gained a lot of extra responsibility after he died.*
>
> *Another hard thing for me was the nature of his*
> *disease. He had brain cancer and was sick for more than*
> *two years before he died. His medication made him regress*
> *in age to the point that he acted like a small child. He*
> *became bitter and hurtful toward my mom and sister and*
> *me. I know it was just the medication and the tumor*
> *itself, but it left me with a lot of negative memories from*
> *before he died. I get frustrated now when I try to*
> *remember him and all I can remember is him being mean*
> *to us, because he wasn't like that at all. He was very laid-*
> *back and loved us all very much.*
>
> *I also just miss doing father-daughter things.*

I wonder about who is going to walk me down the aisle when I get married. Also I decided to go to the same college as my dad, and I often wish that I could share this experience with him. I wish I could ask him how things were when he was here and have him come visit and show me places he used to go.

The bottom line is that one of the most difficult things about loss is the way it changes us and our families. Cassie found her mother's grief to be among the toughest parts of her loss:

Seeing my mom and not being able to help her was really hard for me. I didn't know what to do to ease her pain. I hated lying in bed at night and listening to her cry, knowing there was nothing I could do to ease her sorrows. I hated to see her walk around so sad.

Christmas was always a special time in my family. The first Christmas after he died was exactly a month to the day after he passed away. We got a tree the day before Christmas and my mom had it out of the house Christmas night. It was hard for me, because it was like nothing was special anymore. Everything that held magic for me went with him when he died. It was hard to see her struggle to survive without my dad. She struggled to smile and struggled to keep on living.

Maybe you recognize your own experiences of "what stinks" in the things mentioned so far. Here are some others:

- Holidays
- Birthdays
- Anniversaries
- Finding their stuff
- Seeing their car in the garage
- When friends first find out
- Seeing the other parent cry
- Friends who think you should be over it
- Ongoing bad dreams and nightmares
- When mail comes for them
- Economic change
- Parents taking on an extra role
- People who say stupid stuff
- When people say they wished their parent(s) were deceased
- When people use the word "die" the wrong way
- When you see other kids with their parents
- Going to funeral homes
- Seeing cemeteries
- Coming in contact with things they enjoyed
- Remarriage/Stepfamily
- Family and friends who never got to know the person who died

- Filling out forms
- Being afraid of another loss

Loss can also trigger huge feelings of injustice. Hilary misses the rituals of family life with her father, who died on 9/11. But she also expresses what many teens, whether they've lost a father or a mother, feel at different times on their journey through loss and healing:

> The fact that it is not fair stinks. I appreciated my dad more than anyone. I looked up to him, and I lost him. I know kids [who] don't appreciate their parents half as much as I did, and their dads are still here. My mother and I didn't deserve this. We didn't do anything to make this happen; it just did. It also stinks that I couldn't have stopped this from happening. I know that it is just fate, stinky fate.

Whether a loss has been sudden, as Hilary's was, or comes after a long illness, or is a result of a tragedy, it is never fair. It stinks! Experiencing a loss can also bring up new fears: Will something bad happen to my family again? Why did this happen to me?

The teens I interviewed had many different responses to the question of whether they feared losing other loved ones.

Some acknowledge this fear as "major" but said they try not to think about it. Others answered that this fear was not huge in their lives, and some try to make peace with the fear by accepting that everything happens for a reason.

For 16-year-old Casey, who lost her father when she was 8, the fear of another loss is significant, even years after losing a parent:

> *The thought of losing my mom is my biggest fear. For years after my dad died, I would wake up in the middle of the night, terrified that my mom might have died in her sleep like my dad did, so I would go into her room and make sure she was still breathing.*

Seventeen-year-old Franco was 14 when his father died on 9/11 in the attack on the World Trade Center. His parents were divorced, and he lived with his mother. He told me he doesn't fear losing other loved ones, thanks in large part to his deep faith and his last encounters with his father:

> *My last words to my father over the phone the day before he died were "I love you," and the last time I saw him in person, I gave him a hug. I feel blessed to have had this opportunity, and I believe if God wants me to say good-bye, He will make it possible.*

For Cassie, the idea of not being able to say good-bye if something were to happen to her mother is a fear she and many of the teens I've worked with at CZC live with every day:

I still live in fear every day of losing my mom and my grandma. Losing my dad made me realize that no one is invincible. On Thanksgiving morning, my dad was skipping down the sidewalk, and less then five hours later, he was dying on a stretcher that got rolled down that same sidewalk. Life to me became so fragile. Every day, in the back of my mind, is the fear of losing my mom. I know, realistically, if something happened to her, I would not be able to do anything to stop it. But to make myself feel better, I talk to her every day, just to reassure myself that she's okay. Sometimes when I can't get ahold of her, I get really scared that something happened. I just don't know what I would do if I lost my mom. After my dad died, she and I got extremely close. We're best friends, and I'm not sure if I would be able to handle losing her.

I do fear not being able to say good-bye to my mom. I think, subconsciously, every time I say good-bye, I do it as if it was the last time I was ever going to see or talk to her again. Each time I end a conversation with her, I always say "I love you," because I never know if it is going to be the last time I'll get to tell her. I think it is probably a defense mechanism on my part. So I'm already prepared if something does happen. At least I won't regret saying something to her, which is what happened when my dad died.

As much as we might want to "turn off" the fear of losing another loved one, it's perfectly normal to feel this way. Something horrible has happened to you. After losing a parent, your life isn't the same. Fearing another loss may be difficult to explain to a friend who hasn't gone through what you have, but your surviving parent, a close relative, or a counselor can help you feel safer — if you talk to them. You might have to take the first step (remember, this journey can feel like running a marathon), but it will be worth it.

Since his mother's death, Matt has dealt with his fear of another loss by talking to his father:

Now, having only my dad, I don't know what I'd do if he died. But I think he summed it up pretty well when he said, "You would do what you're doing right now . . . living." And he is right — I would have to go on. It's the way my mom and dad would want it to be.

"Stinky fate," as Hilary called it earlier, can feel pretty scary. After my mother died, and the unthinkable happened and I lost my father too, I felt shattered. But, as Matt's father points out, you have to keep on living your life. I knew that I did. My parents would have wanted me to be okay, but more important, I wanted to be okay. I had lost a big part of my life, and even if I couldn't get my old life back, I wanted to be okay for whatever lay ahead.

There's no easy "cure" for these scary feelings. But having a game plan can help. Talk with your parent and ask what would happen to you if he or she were to die. I know this can be painful. If you don't feel comfortable asking them, put it in a letter or e-mail. Give your input by telling them who you would like to live with. Your parent may be afraid to bring the subject up to you, for fear it may upset you. But keep in mind that it might be a relief for them to talk about this with you. If tears flow during this conversation, because it is a tough one to have, that's okay.

Loss is scary. Fear is a natural response to the loss of a parent. Even though it doesn't always feel like things are in our control, there are ways we can help one another feel safe — driving carefully, making healthy choices about what we eat and drink, calling home if we're out late, and, of course, talking to people we trust about our fears.

✳   ✳   ✳

It *really* stinks when there's trauma or a darker side to the loss and things were left unsaid or undone, or a lot of "unfinished business" is left, along with many unanswered questions. This makes it much harder to move forward. Issues like abuse, suicide, and murder are extra complicated and add additional layers to handling your grief. These are *big* issues for anyone of any age. No one should deal with these things alone. If you are in this situation, please get some help and guidance from a trusted adult so that depression and other obstacles don't stop you from healing.

Sixteen-year-old Peter, who was 12 when his dad committed suicide, says:

Nothing new ever happens — no new trips with my dad, no new memories, and the ones I have are fading. I miss him so much.

I wish someone would have told me that there was a real possibility that my dad was going to kill himself. They all told me it was okay and it's going to be fine. They never once said, your dad might be gone FOREVER. They put false leads in my head, so it was at a total surprise when my dad went missing. I thought it was a joke.

For 14-year-old Brittany, whose father committed suicide when she was 12, the actual act of the suicide is embedded in her mind:

What stinks the most is imagining my dad shooting himself in the head. It makes me sick. I've been wondering what he looked like and if he took it slow or just went right to it. I just don't know. Everything stinks.

Fifteen-year-old Melissa was 12 and in foster care when her mother died of a drug overdose:

What stinks the most is having my friends say to me, "Oh, me and my mom are going shopping after school," or "Oh, I got my mom a really nice necklace for Mother's Day." I really hate it when people say, "I understand," because, well, no, you don't. Did your mother commit suicide? I never did get to say good-bye. I wasn't given the chance to try to help her. That really makes me bitter. I get beyond furious when I think about everything. For starters, the truth would have helped. My foster mother told me that my mother had died from a heart attack. I understand why she told me what she did. But I needed the truth. I wish that someone had told me the reason people were whispering was because they felt awkward and that they didn't know what to say to me. Maybe if I had been told that it wasn't my fault sooner, then I wouldn't still be thinking it was my fault. What I really needed the most was someone to tell me I was not alone. I felt so ashamed and dirty, and I thought that I must not be able to be loved if my mom wanted to kill herself. These are just some of the things that I wish someone had even attempted to explain to me.

Brittany shares these feelings:

I wish that someone had told me about my father's problems. We could have probably gotten help for him, and he wouldn't have killed himself.

When it comes to traumatic loss, 14-year-old Katie responds:

What other kind is there? My dad died on 9/11, but it wouldn't have been any easier if he'd been hit by a truck, except in the way people treat me and my mom.

Well, I've put it out there. Grief does stink. But there is still more to it, isn't there?

3

GRIEF IS . . . LIKE AN EARTHQUAKE

*Grief is like an earthquake. The first one hits you
and the world falls apart. Even after you put the
world together again there are aftershocks,
and you never really know when those will come.*

There is no single definition of grief. It feels different to each
person who experiences it. It changes from day to day, month
to month, and year to year. Sadness, anger, loneliness, numbness, fear, confusion, and even relief are just a few of the
components of grief.

There just isn't a magic "right" way to grieve. Grief doesn't
have an expiration date (although many people who have never
had a loss would like you to think there is one). Grief also
looks different depending on how new or recent your loss.

What does your grief look like? What did it look like in
the beginning? Has it changed?

For me, in the beginning, I remember feeling numb and
functioning like a robot — going through the motions but
not really feeling anything. It was like a bad dream that I
wanted to wake up from but couldn't.

Emily F. was 13 when her father died. Two years later, this is how she describes grief:

> *Grief is like the rain. Sometimes it only drizzles, but other times it pours so much you feel like you're going to drown in it.*

Eighteen-year-old Mary was 10 when she lost her father to cancer. It was complicated by the fact that her parents were divorced and her dad lived out of state. Like Emily F., Mary thinks of rain when describing grief:

> *Grief is like infinite raindrops falling on my skin. Sometimes it feels like the rain will never stop and I will drown in my own grief.*

Grief can definitely feel like a "downpour" (maybe even a tidal wave), especially at the beginning. Your life has changed, and it's difficult to believe that what's happening is real. Then, on top of the "downpour," you may get pressured by family, friends, or relatives to be "brave" or "strong" — advice people often give after someone has died. What does this mean? Eighteen-year-old Elizabeth, who was 12 when her father died, remembers this happening to her:

The adults in my life kept pushing on me the
responsibility to be strong and take care of my mom and
the members of my family. I didn't want to talk to them.
I kept wanting to tell them, "No. This is my loss too!"

Are we really "brave" when we ignore our feelings and act as if our loss didn't happen? Does shutting down our sadness make us "strong"? I think the bravest thing you can do is be real with yourself and feel whatever it is you are feeling. Give yourself permission to let it go — cry, be angry, scream, be scared. Letting go actually is one of the bravest things you can do when you are grieving, especially during the initial "downpours." And when you are ready, talk with people you trust about what you are going through. Tell them what you need. It may be nothing more than a hug or someone just to sit there and listen.

The downpours will lighten eventually.

Elizabeth's family was preparing to move to another town, and their lives were, as she puts it, "turned upside down" by her father's death. Five years later, she recalls how dealing with her loss also involved figuring out what was right for her.

When my dad died, people told me all these things that I
should do — I had journals coming out my ears — but

*nobody told me to figure out what was right for me, what
would help me the most. You can't learn to cope with a
loss based on what other people tell you. You have to do what
makes you happy or what makes you remember or what
makes you feel whole again and go with it without
hesitation. You have to grieve at your own pace.*

I can't say it enough: We all grieve differently. Elizabeth
says it so well: Your grief will happen at your own pace.

Cassie's father died when she was 15. In the two years since
his death, taking time to remember her dad during the "roller
coaster" of grief has helped Cassie ride out the low times:

*Grief to me is like a never-ending roller coaster. Imagine
a roller coaster that is just a series of hills, up and down,
up and down. Sometimes I'm on the top of the hill: being
up there can last for days, sometimes weeks. But then
something little — a memory, a song, a picture — will
trigger emotions that send you flying back down the hill.
And then the only thing you can do is brace yourself, hold
on tight, and go flying down the tracks. Once you hit the
bottom, it's uphill from there. There are times when I feel
myself at the bottom of the hill for a long time. Usually,
it's around a holiday or a special time, like my*

graduation. And it feels like the roller coaster broke and will never start up again. But I just think of happy times with my dad and know that he is watching everything I do from the sky. And then sooner or later, the roller coaster will start up again, and I'll be heading back up the hill. I find that when I start to fly down the hill, the thing that helps is to write or look at pictures of my dad or just talk to him. To get myself back up the hill, I do the same things.

Remembering happier times helped Cassie get that roller coaster moving up the hill again. It's like Emily F.'s comparison of grief to rain. There are times of downpour and times of drizzle. After a while, you will begin to feel that you're turning a corner toward healing. No one can say when that will happen, but it *will* happen. You may realize in the midst of a daily activity — school, sports, taking a shower, or listening to music — it's been five, ten, or even twenty minutes since you last thought about your loss.

All the teens I interviewed had unique and sometimes humorous ways of describing this turning point. Emily S., one of Elizabeth's younger sisters, was 10 when their father died. Now 16, she describes grief in a way all teens can relate to:

Grief is like acne. Because when it comes around it
really sucks, but it's not something that's always there . . .
and it eases up eventually.

Eighteen-year-old Lora was 10 when her father died from a stroke. When I asked her to describe grief, her answer rang true for me and made me smile:

This took some thought, but I'll take a line from **Shrek**
and say it's like an onion (or a parfait!) because it has
multiple layers, and each layer is a little different. And
alone, it is not a pleasant thing, but put with the right
ingredients, like friends, memories, or a support network,
it can turn into an amazing piece of your life. It gives
your life a little flavor!

In referring to grief as something that gives life "flavor," Lora brings up a great point, one that I've found to be true in my own life: You can find yourself a stronger, kinder, and maybe even a better person as a result of your loss. This won't happen right away, but it will come in time. Kurt Stiefvater, a Healing Circle leader, advises teens not to push themselves too hard as they begin to connect with feelings of healing and hope. "Getting through it involves being aware of the small signs that things are getting better — more energy, for example."

The connection with the feeling that your grief is getting "better" can take on many forms. As Kurt points out, you might begin to feel some of your old energy return, which means you might have more energy to reach out and find people you can talk to. Your family and friends might be hesitant to bring up memories of your parent, but if you want to talk about good times, bad times, or just hear a story about your mom or your dad, then let people know you welcome their stories (we'll talk about this more in Chapter 8.) You'll help yourself as well as the person who talks with you.

As you experience the downpours and drizzles of grief, you'll begin to understand that you and those around you who are also affected by your loss experience grief in different ways and at a different pace. Elizabeth has another great way to explain how grief changes over time:

> *It's like a cut. At first it hurts so bad, and you bleed for a while. You stop the bleeding, the pain subsides, and you put on a bandage to hide the mark and help it heal faster. You develop a scab, but every once in a while, that scab might break and you'll bleed again. Once that stops and the pain is gone, you still have a scar. That scar becomes a part of you, and it's something people will know about. It will stay with you for the rest of your life, as will grief.*

Sixteen-year-old Ella, who lost her father in the 9/11 attack on the World Trade Center, sums up the roller-coaster ride of grief's different stages with honest and reassuring words:

> Grief is a process. You go through stages of grief, and everyone's grief is different in both its form and its order. Some people will be angry, then sad, then very depressed, then suddenly be fine. I was scared, then a little bit angry, sad, depressed, okay, depressed, okay, angry, sad, etc. It's a cycle, or a wave. It continues on and on, but it changes periodically. I don't think it ends, but it stops being so prominent in your life.

Matt was 14 when his mother died. He has worked as a junior counselor at CZC and, like Ella, has learned from experience that the grief process is inevitable and unpredictable:

> To any professionals who think they KNOW the grief journey, I beg to differ, because grief is handled by everyone differently. Grief is something that really never ends. It definitely gets better over time, but it always stays with you, and that is not a bad thing. It's great to be able to remember all the good times and even the tough times. But everyone does grieve differently, so however fast you move in your grief process, IT IS THE RIGHT SPEED!

Matt's point about grief bears repeating: Everyone grieves differently. I've heard kids at CZC voice many times and in many ways the pressure they've felt to "get over" their losses and "move on." Kids and teens have it rough — they've been through a life-changing experience, they've suffered an incredible loss, and they're expected to get back into their routines as quickly as possible. You might feel you need to be "strong" for your surviving parent, your siblings, your relatives, and even for your friends. You might feel pressure to grieve in a certain amount of time or in a certain order.

Ed Whitacre, one of our Healing Circle leaders, explains that how a person grieves depends on many things. "Some families and cultures have rituals for grieving that dictate method and length of permitted grieving," he says. "Some folks just express themselves in different ways. . . . Just because a person isn't crying doesn't mean he or she isn't mourning or grieving."

Your loss is with you for the rest of your life. Only you know your "right" way to grieve and your own speed.

Cassie was acutely aware of other people's expectations about her grieving process:

> *I don't think that anyone [gave] me specific time periods of*
> *when I should be doing certain grieving things. But people*
> *have made comments about me not following a normal*
> *routine of grief. I think for the first year I was basically*

surviving on autopilot. But once the numbness wore off and I began to grieve, it was extremely hard for me. I had a tough time concentrating in school, and I was always sad. Teachers started to make comments. I had one teacher tell me that I had no reason to be sad anymore — it had been a year and I should be over it. I had another teacher tell me that my dad dying wasn't an excuse and that I needed to stop being sad and focus. It is so frustrating because there was no "on" or "off" switch. It wasn't like I could turn off the feeling of sadness, even though I wished I could at times. It made me angry because I didn't ask for my dad to die. I wished so hard that I could just be normal, just be able to blend in with everyone else. But losing a parent gives you a label, makes you different, and separates you from the crowd. I remember feeling so helpless because I was getting in trouble for not concentrating, but there was nothing I could do to fix it. His death and the future of my mom and me was always on my mind. People just didn't understand that grief doesn't just disappear, that sadness doesn't just fade away. I wished people would understand that.

Lora was 10 when her father died. Like Cassie, she longed for someone to acknowledge that she needed to grieve in her own time:

Right after my dad died, people would give me books about the grieving process or try and tell me that first I would be mad, then I would be sad, etc. Most people never came out and said anything, but I could tell that people were expecting me to be "more upset" than I acted and were concerned about me. I remember my elementary school guidance counselor saying that people expected me to be crying all the time and that it was okay if I wanted to. I appreciated her telling me that it was okay for me to be upset, but no one ever told me it was okay to want to move on with life and deal with it at my own pace either. My way of grieving was to move on until I was ready to grieve, and I don't think many people saw that.

Hannah was 9 when her father died after battling cancer for three years. While no one told her there was a particular order that the stages of her grieving process should follow, she was aware of the pressure to give grief a deadline:

Some people say you stop grieving after five, ten, or fifteen years, but the truth is it never stops hurting, and you never stop grieving or missing your loved one. When I get married I know I am going to be missing my father a lot because he won't be there to walk me down the aisle or

have that father-daughter dance I have always looked
forward to sharing with him.

Grief can feel like it will never end. It's like a volcano: It can be dormant for a long time and then suddenly explode. If you're going through one of the explosive times, be good to yourself. Cry. Write in your journal. Talk to someone you trust. Paint, or draw, or play music. Try to rest and eat well. Do exercise or sports that make you feel good. Treat your mind, your body, and your heart with care and respect. As our Healing Circle leader Ed says, "If there are 'wrong' ways to grieve or mourn, I would think that would have to do with being stuck in or choosing unsafe or unhealthy ways of expressing oneself." If your grief feels overpowering right now, remember that it will get better. Matt offers some more reassuring words:

> *Grief is like the stock market — one day you're going*
> *up, and you're just as easily on the way down the next*
> *day. But there is always that positive slope that makes it*
> *get better over time.*

Nineteen-year-old Abby O., who was 14 when her mom died from cancer, has made peace with her grief being a permanent part of her:

In the beginning, it was like an invisible cloud hanging over my head with a strange smell: No one could quite see it, but they knew something was up. I could try and ignore it, but it would follow me around. Now it looks like me. It is a part of me, it is all of me, it is always with me, but it doesn't necessarily stick out or smell funny. It is just there, and I am okay with it.

Grief is the key to healing. Sometimes you have to walk through that "wall of pain" to get to the other side of healing. I know it's difficult to believe that experiencing pain will help you heal, but it works. I wrote earlier that when you finish this book, you might feel as if you've run a marathon. By reading this far, you have crossed the starting line and are officially in the race. Keep going. Pace yourself. You can do it! Remember, you are not on this journey alone.

4

EVERY LOSS IS UNIQUE

I had no idea what was going to happen. . . .

Every loss is unique, from who was lost to how the person died. Someone whose mom died suddenly might wish to have prepared for her death the way another person did whose father was terminally ill. But the person who watched his dad suffer a long illness might wish he hadn't seen his father so sick.

I've participated in many of these discussions with kids at camp. When talking about sudden loss and death from long-term illness and which type of loss is easier, campers are really respectful and interested to hear how the other side is coping. They thoughtfully ask questions: "Do you think it was easier knowing your dad was going to die? Did you get to say good-bye?" Then there is the flip side: "Were you glad they didn't have to suffer?" The debate is interesting, but there is no clear answer and no clear winner. No matter what, it still stinks either way.

Some kids hated witnessing the decline of long-term illness and losing a piece of their loved one every day. Some avoided going in their loved one's room; they stopped bringing friends over. It is especially hard if a parent's personality starts to change from the illness or medication. Some campers talk about feeling guilty for avoiding the loved one or feeling relief after they died. Some kids fear "catching" what the loved one had. There were also some beautiful instances of dying gracefully, when the loved one said their good-byes, when vigils were held and favorite songs were sung.

Teens who lost their parent or parents through a sudden loss often express how they never feel fully safe again. There is a lingering fear of always waiting for the "other shoe to drop," the knowledge that your world could be ripped apart in an instant. Simple things like your surviving parent being late to pick you up, strange cars in the driveway, or even a phone call from a relative, make your mind instantly go to "Did someone else die?"

I remember walking home from high school with my brother Matt. I was a junior and he was a senior. We had almost gotten to our house when we saw a bunch of strange cars in our driveway. We both stopped walking at exactly the same time. My heart started beating a little faster. I said to him, "You know any time I see cars in the driveway and I don't know whose they are, I always think someone else has died." Matt said, "I know. I always think the same thing too." We walked slowly into the house, only to find my stepmother hosting a bridge game.

Ed Whitacre, a Healing Circle leader, has these observations to offer when it comes to both types of losses:

*I think the biggest difference between death from a long-
term illness and sudden death is that in the long-term
illness case we have the chance to prepare for our loved
one's dying, and in the other case we don't.*

*When I say "prepare," I mean being able to do things
like making sure you say the things you want to say,
talking about what death means and how you feel about
it, sharing memories, asking questions, making amends
for old hurts, and talking about future hopes and dreams.
I think these are things that we should do no matter
which kind of death scenario it is, and we can do these
things with our surviving loved ones and friends, even if
we don't get the chance to do it with the one who is dying.*

*My own father's death was sudden in that we didn't
know how ill he was, and his cancer took him in one
week. I was 15. I remember wishing I could have said
good-bye or been there to see him go. I felt very cheated.
I remember thinking that maybe he didn't really die and
that, for some reason, he was sent away somewhere. I've
also talked with folks who described having had bad
arguments or having had bad feelings with the person
who died suddenly, ones that never got resolved. I think
that with sudden deaths we are more vulnerable to
feelings of guilt and anger at what should or shouldn't*

have been done and of disbelief or denial that it really happened.

This is not to say that, in either scenario, you are necessarily more vulnerable to certain feelings than in the other. In both cases, there can still be sadness, anger, guilt, numbness, relief, confusion, denial, etc. There can still be thoughts of "I should have said . . . should have done . . . if only . . ." And we still will worry about the loved ones around us and about what may happen to them. Sometimes, even if we know someone is going to die, it is hard to do the things to prepare ourselves for it. Perhaps we are afraid to burden others with our thoughts or we don't want to see others get upset.

All the things I've described that prepare us for someone's impending death are the things we need to do as part of mourning anyway. Mourning helps us stay connected to the person who died. It helps us make sense of what is or what has happened. It helps to express or channel, in a positive way, all the feelings that come with death, and we need to express or channel them somehow so we don't get stuck. By doing the "prepare" things, either before or after the death, you get a chance to hear what others feel and think, and that can help you make sense of your own feelings and thoughts, even if

another person's may be different. Doing these things
makes it real.

Thinking about the way in which your parent died is
normal and just a part of sorting through your loss. Even if
your loss occurred some time ago, you might still be wondering if your loved one felt pain, was scared, or was at peace. You
might also wonder if it will happen to you. It's natural to
believe that some deaths are "better" or "worse" than others,
especially as you deal with the trauma of losing your parent.
By reading the ways teens describe what was unique to their
losses, I hope you'll connect with some of their experiences
and arrive at new insights about your own loss.

Katie, whose dad died on 9/11, expresses thoughts that
anyone who has experienced a sudden loss has likely shared:

I had no idea about what was going to happen and no
time to prepare. Sometimes I wonder if knowing
beforehand would have helped at all.

Hilary describes the particular pain of 9/11:

9/11 was just like any other day; I never expected it to
change my life forever. I was in shock when I heard that

the towers had collapsed. My life hasn't been the same since and never will be. I'd like to think that my dad just vaporized and didn't know what hit him. It is strange because there is no grave, so it's not like it's final.

Ella also lost her father on 9/11, and she touches on how that very public event makes her experience — and that of many other kids who lost parents during the attacks — different:

With the traumatic events surrounding 9/11, the situation and his death were much more hyped up than maybe a more natural cause would have been. Not being able to have much physical evidence also means I still don't really have closure.

Emily S., whose father died suddenly from heart failure while jogging, mourns not having been able to say good-bye:

My loss was very sudden, and I always wish I could have had one last chance to talk to my dad and tell him that I love him very much. I did not have to watch him suffer, but I wish that I could have had some warning so that the loss wouldn't have come as such a shock.

Perhaps because she is the oldest, Emily's sister Elizabeth also mourns not having had the chance to say good-bye but feels other stresses:

My dad's death was sudden, so we had no chance to say good-bye to him or have any closure with our relationship. Also, we were supposed to be moving in just a couple of weeks, and our lives were already turned upside down as it was. We then had to readjust to the idea that we weren't going anywhere and fight to keep our house. It was a very traumatic and stressful experience for my whole family.

Change is inevitable after a parent dies — there is a hole in your family that was not there before. You may find yourself worrying about money, your household, moving, or changing schools. You may even wonder what will happen to you if your surviving parent should die. It's natural to worry. Consider having a conversation with your surviving parent or close relatives. It helps to talk openly with your family about different options and what to expect. You have a right to be in the loop. These changes affect you too. Answers to these questions will help you rebuild your sense of safety and security.

It may seem difficult to revisit happy times with your loved one after suddenly losing them, but your memories can provide safety and solace. Sixteen-year-old Casey's father was an airline pilot and was away from home when he died of a heart attack. Casey was 8 when her father died, and all these years later she too wishes she could have said good-bye. But she also expresses how her good memories help her deal with his sudden death:

> It was difficult never saying good-bye. There are so many things that I wish I could have said to him before he died. But at the same time, I'm glad that my last memory of him was not of him lying sick in a hospital bed, but instead it was just us in our everyday lives, laughing and having fun.

Matt not only had to deal with sudden, horrible news but also with a painful decision:

> My mom died suddenly from a brain aneurysm. I was working at a golf course, and my dad called me and told me to come home with my neighbor (who also worked at the golf course). At the hospital, my dad told me what happened, and we as a family made the decision to take her off life support. It was the toughest decision we have ever made.

Fourteen-year-old Beth also found herself in a tough situation, which she now feels grateful for:

My dad was sick for quite a while with a brain tumor. One thing that is unique to my loss is that I was the only person in the room when my dad died. I feel so grateful because I was the last one to see him before he left my family.

Melissa's mother committed suicide two years ago. This circumstance, plus the fact that she hadn't seen her mother before she died, brought a sense of shock that Melissa continues to experience:

My mother committed suicide when I was in a foster home. It was a Sunday morning, and I hadn't seen my mother for a few weeks because she kept saying she was feeling "sick." I thought that she had been drinking and smoking and that this was why she wasn't keeping up with the weekly visitations that we were supposed to have on Mondays.

While I was in foster care, I was always on guard. By saying that, I mean that you always had to be prepared for the unexpected. My foster mother told my sister and me that she needed to talk to us after breakfast. So what I did was go and start packing my bags because when you're in foster care you move around a lot. However, in reality, when we had our little talk it wasn't about leaving but about staying. I had made my mother a really nice card with hearts and other things too. I was so excited to see her and tell her everything I had been up to. But that never happened, and she never got her card.

Everything was supposed to be getting better, and we were supposed to be able to go home soon. I was in shock for quite some time. I'm still in shock.

Cassie found meaning in her actions as she witnessed her father's sudden death from a heart attack:

I never got to say good-bye to my dad. There were so many things left unsaid when he passed away. There were so many things I wish we had talked about. I know a lot about his life, but I don't know everything and I never will. It came out of nowhere, and it was a shock to my family. It hit us unexpectedly, and it made it harder to grieve. It took me a lot longer to acknowledge the fact that he was gone because I kept saying that it didn't happen. I was in total shock because of the suddenness of my loss.

I had to watch my dad pass away in front of my eyes. It is something I will never forget. Running in and seeing *him on the floor is an image that is forever embedded in my brain. I'll never forget the events of that day and how I tried to hold onto his foot as someone pulled me away from him. Now that I look back, it was symbolic; I was trying to hold on, as an invisible force was pulling him out of my grasp.*

After a sudden loss, it's natural to fantasize about ways in which we might have "held on." Not having the closure of saying good-bye can be especially tough. Saying good-bye *after* the death may seem weird, bizarre, abstract, impossible, or even dumb. That being said, it can be done, and it can be really helpful in your healing. One of the most powerful activities we do at CZC is releasing balloons into the sky. Campers write notes to their loved ones, attach the notes to helium-filled balloons, and then we gather to release the balloons and watch them float upward carrying our messages to our loved ones. Campers who continue this on birthdays, anniversaries, Mother's Day, Father's Day, or other special days find balloon releases to be a surprisingly powerful way to feel connected to the person they've lost and to begin to let go of the weight of things left unsaid. Even the CZC adult volunteers who are many years past the loss of a parent tell me how meaningful balloon releases are for them.

While many of the teens I surveyed regretted not having had the chance to say good-bye to those they lost suddenly, teens whose parents died after long illnesses express the things that are painful about this kind of death and echo the feelings of helplessness that come with any kind of loss. Suzanne was in elementary school when her father was struck with cancer. As young as she was, she still remembers how it felt during the almost two years of his illness:

> *My dad got sick at the end of my first-grade year, was*
> *sick during most of second grade, then died right before*
> *I started third grade. It was hard because those are the*
> *years when you are supposed to be spending time with*
> *your daddy. [But] he was always sick, so sometimes*
> *I feel like I lost a part of my childhood.*

Hannah was 9 when her father died. Like Suzanne's dad, her father also suffered a long illness. Though he lived for several years while ill, Hannah's description of that time is laced with helplessness:

> *My father lived with a brain tumor for four years. The*
> *doctors said, when he was first diagnosed, that he would*
> *only live for three months. Well, his three months turned*
> *into four years, and I could not be more thankful for that*
> *extended time. It was truly a blessing.*
>   *The worst part about a long-term death is the*

anticipation of the death. It's the scariest feeling in the
world. Watching him slowly begin to lose his senses
and speech due to the cancer in his brain made me feel
helpless. That was the worst feeling in the world.

Abby O., whose mother died from cancer when she was
14, expresses the feeling of relief and then guilt about feeling
relief:

When my mother finally died after being sick for almost
two years, I was relieved, and this made me feel so guilty.
I wasn't relieved that she had died, but I was relieved
that I wouldn't have to see her so sick anymore. I was
guilty then, and I still am, but I understand more now
that it is okay to feel this way.

Losing a Dad vs. Losing a Mom

Whether you've lost your mom or dad, your loss is different
from anyone else's. After my mother died, I missed having her
guidance about the "girl" things we shared that were just ours,
since I didn't have any sisters. But I also missed the father-

daughter moments I had with my father. It was painful to be the only kid in school who didn't have a mom and dad — no one to come watch the cheerleading squad, tennis team, award ceremonies, or my graduation. Teens, both male and female, talk at camp about missing their parents at events that they previously shared as a family: sports, dance, performances, swim meets, and plays.

At CZC, most campers share that in their families, dads often represent the "strong, safe, invincible" guy. Something happening to your dad can really rock your safety net. Dad is often the main breadwinner too, so losing him can mean that finances are lost, or your mom may have to go to work, or sometimes you have to move to a different or smaller house. Mom going back to work means you lose the roles you are used to her filling, from carpooling to being home when you get home from school. So the loss of a father can be almost a dual loss. And if you are male, you have lost that person to teach you and do "guy stuff" with.

Franco lost his father on 9/11. He describes what he misses the most about his dad:

> *Not being able to talk with my father about things my mom wouldn't care for and experiencing them with his perspective in mind.*

Peter, 16, whose dad committed suicide when he was 12, echoes those same sentiments:

> *Not only did I lose my dad, I lost my best friend, my mentor, my teacher, my history, his secrets. I lost all the things a dad teaches a son.*

Losing a male role model is not only difficult for guys. Emily S. mentioned in the last chapter how much she missed playing sports with her dad, since he'd been her soccer coach. Her older sister, Elizabeth, feels their loss in a different way:

> *The fact that my house is now all girls was a really big change. My dad added a lot to our lifestyle just by being a guy, and now all that is totally different.*

Casey misses her father's influence:

> *My dad was supposed to be my protector and keep me safe. My dad used to be the laid-back, easygoing one, and now the only one I have is my mom, who is much more uptight. My dad was supposed to take me camping and fishing and teach me all the guy stuff.*

Ella, who lost her father on 9/11, misses his personality and the two-parent dynamic. She also touches on what so many teens discuss at camp — the sometimes jarring ways in which we are reminded of our loved ones:

> I lost the cuddly, run-to-when-Mom-is-mad, affectionate, easygoing guy who I depended on and trusted for everything. I still look for him in the little blue type of cars that he drove, or I see a big guy and do a double take. That is hard.

Hilary also lost her dad on 9/11, and misses their closeness:

> It is weird not having a dad because he was the guy I could always count on to have fun with. He was the one who helped me with homework or who I could talk about sports with. Even though he worked a lot, he was one of my best friends. When I lost him, I lost my father and my friend.

Caitlin, 13, wonders about starting high school, and she worries about how it will feel to stay in a place to which her father, who died when she was 7, was closely connected:

He was the principal at the county high school, and now
I start to wonder if I can go to [that] high school
without getting upset. For now I can go to football games
but staying at my father's high school may bring back
memories.

Now that Hannah is a teenager, her feelings about her father's death have taken on a new meaning. Her concise description is one that many teens ponder as they get older:

He died when I was 9. Sometimes I feel like I didn't
really get to know him.

The loss of a mother, who is typically the nurturer and the glue that holds the family together, is devastating. It's shattering for young children and teens alike to lose the person who keeps the house running, knows what meals you like and just how to make them, makes sure you have clean clothes and new clothes when you need them, is the one who comforts you when you're sad and sick, and is there for you when you just want to share a great moment. Even the toughest guys may mourn the loss of the nurturing or "mothering" they may still only secretly admit that they like. Girls lose the role model who teaches them the how-to's of being a woman. I've heard time and time again from campers that an added challenge after losing a mother is that dads often start dating right away and tend to remarry within about two years. Campers share that their fathers think that "getting a woman in the house" will restore the family's balance.

Matt misses his mother's nurturing and her career experience, especially as he begins to explore his own career path:

> *She was always a great cook. I know that's a weird thing to miss, but she could cook. I always enjoyed her stories from the hospital (she was a nurse). I would talk for hours with her about all of her patients. It was a cool little bond we had, and that has led me to wanting to be a doctor.*

Brianna, 14, lost her mom ten years ago and still misses her today:

> *I lost my mom at the age of 4 and have never stopped thinking about her since then. I know that I didn't know her that well, but I miss her so much and now I live with my dad and two brothers, and I don't really have anyone to talk to about girl things.*

Abby O. also misses the presence of a mother to confide in:

I don't have anyone to talk about girl stuff with, and I feel
like I don't know a lot of the basic things that women should
know (how to write thank-you notes, put together a dinner
or an outfit, throw an elegant party). It's funny, because my
mom was an international diplomat, so she had to know how
to do all these things, but they were the least important part
of her life. They really stick out for me though.

Matt's younger sister, Amy, 14, who was 11 when their
mom died, agrees:

Just thinking about not having a mom stinks the most.
Now that I have lost my mom, I have to do "girl things"
with my dad. Since my mom's death, it has been hard to
really "grow up." Mother's Day is always hard. People
always ask me, "What did you get for your mom?" It's
hard because I see girls walking with their moms, and
I think how wonderful it would be just to have my
mom back.

These reflections of feeling awkward or that other women
(who have mothers) "have the key" to womanhood that I did
not get ring true for me even today. I still struggle with female
things like going to baby and wedding showers for which I
agonize over buying the right present, feel like the present isn't

wrapped as nicely as the others, wonder if I am wearing the right thing. I often feel like I have a neon sign over my head that says something like, "I don't have a mother. I don't belong with the rest of you." What helps me now is telling either the person who invited me or a friend who will also be in attendance that showers are challenging for me. That "depowers" the feelings. I also try to plan to do something nice for myself after a shower or all-girl event to pick myself up.

There are very few books for kids and teens on parent loss, and most I've seen focus on the loss of a mother or a father but never acknowledge that some kids may have lost both parents. It doesn't happen often, but it does happen. One of the things that was hardest for me about losing both of my parents is that I never got to know them as people — as Marilynn and Skip. I only knew them as Mom or Dad. I don't know if I'm like them, and if I am, in what way. You lose a huge part of their legacies and your family's history.

John, 15, lost both of his parents within a year when he was 14. He now lives with his aunt and uncle. He says what was unique for him about losing both parents is "not being able to ask either one of my parents questions about themselves and their lives during my early childhood."

The death of both parents is a child or teen's worst nightmare. If this has happened to you, you may feel, as I did, that your entire personality has changed, and that your world has shattered. I want you to know that, although your circumstances are extra complex and challenging, you can still survive, and you can still lead a happy life. It is going to take work, and you are going to have to be your own advocate and cheerleader and look out for yourself. You can do it. I'm proof it can be done!

5

FEELING DIFFERENT FROM OTHERS

I understand what it means to lose someone. . . .

Our society puts a lot of pressure on us to get over our losses. They give you six months, maybe a year. After someone dies, we're expected to pick up where we left off and almost immediately get back to our day-to-day routines. "Going through the motions" can feel healing: School, sports, work, and social activities can be great opportunities to step out from under the weight of loss, even for a little while.

One thing's for sure, though — life is not the same after the loss of a parent. In addition to all the huge changes we've already discussed, another common theme is feeling different from your friends and other kids your age. It's a feeling that may change over time but doesn't really ever go away. However, the good news is that it doesn't always feel terrible either. Talking about it is one way you can feel less isolated from others. Sometimes this means honest conversations with your friends. Other times it means finding someone outside your circle of friends who will listen.

Every teen I interviewed for this book answered yes when I asked if they feel different from other kids. Their explanations of how they feel different include a unanimous feeling of being "older" and more mature than their peers. Cassie felt this most strongly when she went back to school soon after her father died:

> When I went back to school after my dad died, I felt the difference between the other kids and me. When I was sad and I cried, they looked at me differently. I almost felt like I was in another league. I was no longer on equal ground with them. I was dealing with something that none of them had ever experienced, and it separated me from them.

Hilary says she feels 50 years old, "easily":

> It is so weird. I feel like I have grown up prematurely. When my friends do something stupid, it's like I'm their mother and I'm telling them what's right and wrong.

Melissa shares how confusing it feels to have to grow up suddenly:

> I feel a lot older than I am. I used to only want to hang out with all the seniors at school, and I wouldn't talk to anyone my age. I always thought they were too immature. I

sometimes feel like I'm 15, and other times I feel like I
should be a college student. But then there are times when
I try to act like my little sister. I never got to be a little kid
because I had to act older than I was when I was younger.
I had to take care of my mom when she was drunk. So
sometimes I still want to be a parent even though I am in
a situation where I can be a normal teenager.

Suzanne also mourns for the childhood she feels she lost out on:

I often feel older than my friends because I have felt and
experienced more than they have. But sometimes I feel
really young and naive because I never really got to have
a childhood because my dad was sick for most of it.

Casey, Beth, Peter, and Ella agree that since their losses they too feel older than other kids:

Some days, I feel like a normal 16-year-old, but others I
feel 50 years old walking around with this huge burden on
my shoulders that I have to deal with.   — Casey

I am not sure how old I feel. I do know, though, that I
skipped many of my childhood years. I feel that I am more
mature than my friends, and I can handle problems that

*they cannot. I also feel that if I were to live on my own,
within a week, I would be able to because I have so many
responsibilities at home. I also have to take care of myself
more than my friends do. I have to buy clothes and pay for
outings to the movies, dinner with a friend, or anything
that is considered something fun that I want to do.*

— Beth

*It varies, how old I feel. When I forget my problems,
I feel like I'm 10, but when I feel down and am
thinking about my dad, I feel like I'm 80.* — Peter

*Sometimes I feel like I am 5, and I just want to crawl
into my mother's lap, staying there, curled up, oblivious and
ignorant to the rest of the world. At other times I feel so
worn out and so sad, like I've experienced too much to take
anymore. I feel like I'm 80. The thing is, though, that
sometimes all of that doesn't have to do directly with my
dad's death. As a teenager, life is so difficult (especially for
our generation and the upcoming generations) that my dad
dying is just one more thing added to the chaos and turmoil
in my life. At times I'm not upset about it directly, but it's
always on the back burner, and it's one more thing that I
have to deal with.* — Ella

As Ella says, dealing with the loss of a parent is even more difficult on top of the chaos and turmoil of being a teenager. Like Beth, you may have more responsibilities than your friends or money may be tighter in your household.

As I said earlier, I had a hard time being around other kids my age and laughing at what they were laughing at and pretending to worry about what they were worrying about. I wasn't able to let myself go and be silly like other kids my age. That wasn't safe for me. My daily goals revolved around trying be *okay* — not even happy but just *okay* — and make it through each day without crying. For the most part, I felt like I was a 60-year-old, mature beyond my years, but at the same time I somehow missed out on learning basic things that other kids my age knew how to do but no one had ever shown me (pump gas, ask for help in a store, cook a can of corn — so many things!).

As tough and unfair as this forced maturity may be, there is a flip side: You gain an appreciation for those you do have in your life, and you don't take things or people for granted. It makes you appreciate the gift of life. It often makes you closer to the people you love. You gain a sensitivity to other people's pain and challenges too.

Emily S. says she definitely feels different from other kids at school, but that this serves her in positive ways:

I understand what it means to lose someone, and I know how to appreciate people, because they could be gone the next day. I also feel much more mature than most people at my school. Rather than just worrying about clothes and boys, I feel like I have a better perspective on life.

Emily's sister Elizabeth has also gained perspective:

I feel older [than other kids], as far as mind-set and maturity. Kids who haven't been through this focus on a lot of petty things that, in the grand scheme of things, really aren't that important. I guess other kids are ignorant in a way. I don't think any less of them for it; ignorance is something that can't be helped. I just feel that I have a better concept of how devastating life can be in comparison to those who haven't had a tremendous obstacle to overcome.

Hannah agrees that since her father died her outlook on what's important in life has changed:

I am very different from other kids. Since the death of my father, I have matured faster than anyone I have met my own age. This experience made me realize that I

shouldn't sweat the small stuff, because in the long run, it
doesn't really matter. It made me realize that I need to be
thankful for the people who have helped me though these
tough times and cherish them.

Matt and others echo these sentiments. While some of
the following responses overlap, I truly believe you can't hear
often enough that you aren't alone in feeling different:

I, along with anyone else who experiences a loss, am a
part of a unique club. Anyone in this club knows true
pain. This pain forces us to grow up faster than any of
our friends, and therefore makes us much more mature as
we enter middle and high school.   — Matt

I definitely feel like I'm more mature than most 19-
year-olds. Mature in that I recognize how precious life is,
and I know what loss feels like. I had to grow up faster
than most kids my age, and with that comes more
responsibility. I'm definitely more aware of what my
mom does for me and what I can do for her. I think in
high school I was one of the only kids I knew who
appreciated my family so much. I just recognized it
sooner than most kids, I guess.   — Emily L.

My loss has taught me important coping skills and life skills. Even though at times I can get caught up in all the stupid stuff, like boys and clothes, I know there are some things so much more important in life, like people you love, which many kids my age have not figured out yet.

— Casey

I rarely complain about my family like most other teenagers do.   *— Emily S.*

I think I take death more seriously than some other kids. I don't feel immortal. I know that people close to me could die, and I could too.   *— Katie*

In a way, I can be more mature at times or I can be a lot more silly from just finally letting it all out.

— Caitlin

Hilary agrees with many of these teens. While she feels the loss of a "normal" life since her father's death, she has also figured out a way to feel as if he is with her:

Now I appreciate things more. Things that I just took for granted before are becoming really important to me, like my mom. I've also grown up so much from losing my dad. Sure, I would like to be a normal kid again, but I can't. I have to think of the fact that my dad can't tell me what to do, but he is definitely watching my every move from heaven, just seeing if I am using my brain and what he taught me. It is like having a parent with you wherever you go.

Heaven also plays a role in the way that Lora, who was 10 years old when her father died, feels different:

I had to grow up faster and deal with emotions they've never been through. I sometimes feel like I have more respect for life and how fragile it is, so I don't take a lot of the risks that kids my age do. Also I think I have a stronger faith in heaven than most kids my age.

Perhaps you too find comfort in your faith. Comfort Zone Camp is not aligned with any one faith or affliated with any religious organizations, and the campers are children and teens of all religious and ethnic backgrounds. However, many of the teens spoke so openly and eloquently about their faiths that I decided to ask them to elaborate on what part, if any, faith plays in their healing.

Cassie describes her faith as being in "limbo" after her father died:

Right after he passed away, I couldn't talk about anything relating to God or heaven. It made me angry to hear that he was in a better place in heaven, because I was so miserable down here without him and I wanted him back. I was really upset at God too, because I didn't understand why He would take away my dad. But once I got over being angry at Him and realized that everything happens for a reason, it became a lot easier to talk about my faith. Of course, that didn't happen for a few years. During those years when I was in limbo with my faith, I constantly battled over my feelings. But now I'm able to talk about God and my faith with certain people that I trust.

God plays a pretty important role in my life today. I pray to God almost every night. I ask Him to watch over my family and watch over my dad in heaven. Being able to lie in bed at night and just talk to Him about how I was feeling made me feel better. It took some of the weight that I had been carrying around off my chest. Just believing in God gave me hope for the future. I firmly believe that everything is done for a reason, and that God does not give you anything you can't handle . . . that helped me, knowing that God obviously needed my dad for something up in heaven.

For Casey, faith has provided comfort, but it is also something she continues to reexamine:

*I can talk about my faith, even though I'm not quite sure
what that is yet. For the first couple years after my loss, I
became much more religious because I had to believe that
there was a God and a heaven. I had to believe that I
would see my dad again eventually. For a while, that's the
only thing that kept me going. But now that I'm older,
I've actually started to try and figure out what I believe,
even if it might mean looking at the possibility that I
may never see my dad again. God has helped me deal
with my loss by giving me the hope of a higher power
that won't give me more than I can handle.*

In the four years since her father died, Emily L., 19, has
continued to depend on her faith as a way to explore a deeper
meaning to her loss:

*God has been faithful to me through the entire process of
losing my father. I know lots of people get angry at God for
taking away their fathers, but I trust that God does not
want to hurt me like that. My father's passing was part of
God's plan for his life, my mom's life, my sister's life, my life,
and anyone else's life that my father touched. I believe that
my father found life in the Lord through his dying. He was
not a Christian until he had cancer and maybe that was the
Lord's way of getting my dad to heaven. I wish it didn't have*

to be that way, but who am I to question God's plan? This is
not to say that I am okay with not having a dad. My dad's
dying sometimes makes me question if God is fair, and I
wonder why that had to happen to me. Even through that
process, though, my faith has been strengthened immensely.

Our Healing Circle leaders recognize faith as a factor in grieving. Whether you're finding comfort in your faith or are just plain angry at "stinky fate," you too might be looking more closely at the role faith plays in your life after loss. Healing Circle leader Helen Henrich observes that for many people, "the capacity to pray when all seems hopelessly lost is an important coping skill." Kurt Stiefvater, another Healing Circle leader, notes that questions of faith might arise after loss even if religion isn't a regular part of a family's life. "Sometimes in our Healing Circles, teens share stories about feeling the presence of a loved one. For some, this is creepy, but for others, it is quite comforting. Some find answers in religion and feel a greater sense of connection with others who are suffering."

As I've mentioned elsewhere in this book, it may be helpful for you to seek guidance from your pastor, rabbi, priest or other clergy. Questioning your faith after losing a parent doesn't mean you've lost your trust in a higher power forever. You might find you reconnect with your spirituality and faith in entirely different ways.

6

CHANGES AT HOME

*No matter how normal we tried to make our family
seem, life would be altered forever.*

Just as you have been transformed by your grief, your family
will also be. Did you lose the parent you felt closest to? Are
your siblings dealing with the loss in ways that you're not?
And if you don't have siblings, how does that feel? Each member of your family will react and change in different ways
from the exact same loss. Your family will develop new routines, rituals, and ways of relating to each other.

Life after the loss of a parent means a significant reshift-
ing of your family: You, your siblings, and your surviving
parent may have to take on new responsibilities. There are
deep emotional adjustments that come with these shifts too.
At CZC, I have gotten to know not only grieving teens but
their parents as well as their younger brothers and sisters when
they come to camp. When I asked teens about how their relationship with their surviving parent had changed, I got a lot of
different answers. Many said their relationships had shifted
toward more closeness and more trust.

After losing her dad, Hilary, an only child, experienced a new closeness with her mom:

> [We] have a stronger bond. It could have gone either
> way — we could have been like two peas in a pod or we
> could have become strangers to each other. I guess I'm
> lucky; we are like best friends now. My mom is always
> saying we are a team and we have to stick together. It is
> the truth; sometimes parents can be annoying, but no
> matter what, they've always got your back.

Other teens who shared their stories for this book have had experiences similar to Hilary's. Cassie also expresses the ways in which her loss brought her closer to her mother:

> I've learned to appreciate her more. When my dad passed
> away, it was a kick in the stomach. My perfect world
> where my parents were invincible was shattered. I learned
> the reality that no one is invincible. I don't take my mom
> for granted anymore, and that has made our relationship
> stronger. I am more considerate of her. Because my dad
> died early in my teen years, I never went through the huge
> blowout fights with my parents. I think it's because I knew
> my mom was doing the best she could, and I understood
> what she was dealing with, because I was dealing with the

same things. My mom is my best friend now. Once my
dad died, it was just her and me, on our own. I leaned on
her and she leaned on me. We shared this mutual loss, and
it brought us closer together. We were able to talk to each
other about what we were feeling.

Elizabeth also speaks of becoming closer to her mother at the age when many of her peers have begun to pull away from their parents:

I spend a lot of time talking to her — I tell her pretty
much everything. I don't know if that really has to do
with losing my dad, but I know that I appreciate her
more than most kids appreciate their moms. I have a lot
of respect for her because she kept our family together
through my dad's death.

"Keeping the family together" is a key concern among the majority of CZC teens. Losing a parent can bring up worries about money, of course, especially if that parent was the family's main breadwinner. But this loss can also spark worries and frustrations about everyday practical matters that you may never have had to pay attention to before. When Matt's mother died, his dad had to learn to do "mom" things, such as cooking, cleaning, doing laundry for the family, and helping Matt's younger sister through teenage "girl stuff." And if it's Mom who is learning to do "dad" things, such as repairing things, changing electrical fuses, or playing sports, the same concerns might arise. Who will take care of you (or the house, the car, the grocery shopping) now that the parent who handled these things is gone?

Hilary, who is an only child, talks about how much things changed after her dad died on 9/11:

> *I have grown up quickly because I have to share all the housework and things that have to be done with my mom. I have to be strong and able to live on my own without depending on other people to take care of me. It was hard, especially right after 9/11; I tried to take care of everyone except myself. I couldn't cry in front of my mom because I didn't want to make her sad. It was up to my mother and me to do everything. We couldn't wait for someone else to do it because it wouldn't get done.*

It's okay to feel concerned about these and other issues. Try to be patient as your parent figures out his or her new roles. As Hilary says, the bottom line is they've got your back.

You may even find that your family dynamic still feels pretty "normal." Franco, whose father died on 9/11, describes a relationship that is more universal among all teens than specific to teens who have lost a parent:

> *My relationship is up and down with my mom. But I see*
> *it as a typical teen-parent relationship — I want one*
> *thing, she wants another. She's the parent, so I'm supposed*
> *to listen, yada yada yada.*

Losing a parent can bring a close relationship closer, but it can also forge new paths. Fourteen-year-old Beth was 8 when her father died of cancer. Her description of her relationship with her mother now is different from that of most of the teens who responded:

> *When my father was alive, my mother and I were not*
> *close. Since he passed away, I have felt that we have grown*
> *farther apart. At first I actually blamed her for my*
> *father's death, but I understand now that it was not her*
> *fault. When I say that we were not close when my father*
> *was alive, I mean that I was just "Daddy's little girl."*
> *My mom and I are different in the way we process day-*
> *to-day things that come up. She thinks that I must do*
> *everything in my life the way she would, although I have*
> *learned that no two people are alike. My mother and I do*

get along sometimes, though, and we do have our moments
when we are best friends.

Beth's loss occurred when she was much younger, and as a teenager, she has come to accept that she and her mom are different and appreciate the moments they can be "friends."

Abbey H. was 14 when her mother, the parent she was closest to, died:

Dad and I have gotten somewhat closer, but we still will
never be as close as my mom and I were. We don't really
discuss her death that much; it's pretty painful for him to
talk about it. I try my best to make him proud of me and
not make him worry.

Melissa has chosen not to have a relationship with her dad:

I do not speak to my father because he lost custody many
years ago. I am angry at him because he didn't bother to
come to my mother's funeral. I thought he might have the
decency to do that.

Emily L., whose father died when she was 15, describes the challenges of "friendship" with a surviving parent and how she has worked at both mourning and accepting the different terms of her relationship with her mother:

My mom and I are much closer. She had a hard few years after my dad died. I found myself taking care or feeling like I had to take care of her a lot. Through that, we have really learned to trust each other with anything. She's more like a friend than a mom. It's nice now that I'm older to have that relationship, but sometimes I feel like I need a mom and not a friend. She often asks me for advice on work or dating or my sister. She doesn't really have anyone else her age to talk to about these things because she always used to talk to my dad. I often don't feel like it's "normal" to have these conversations with her, and sometimes it makes me really uncomfortable. I've been able to communicate that to her though, and I love her for who she is and wouldn't change her.

Perhaps you too have suddenly found yourself in the "uncomfortable" position of taking care of your surviving parent. Or maybe you may feel driven to take on this responsibility simply because it feels like the right thing to do, and you want to make things easier on your mom or dad. Talking about your feelings may give your parent the opportunity to reassure you that you don't have to fill this role. Healing Circle leader Ed Whitacre was in his teens when he lost his father. Ed points out that "even if there are strong adults around, it's natural [for teens] to be concerned about the welfare and feelings of others in the family. I took on a caretaking role when my father died, but it was never expected of me, and I had no doubts about my mother's ability to take care of us. But I was aware of a void, and I felt some responsibility to fill it. I had no resentment about this, but worry did go with the role. It felt good that my mom acknowledged this at times."

Helen Henrich, a CZC Healing Circle leader, notes it is natural to feel a range of emotions after loss, including resentment over how family dynamics change and sadness that your surviving parent is grieving too. It can be scary to see your mom or dad show these new, strong emotions. Your surviving parent also needs to grieve, and the more in touch they are with their feelings, the more able they'll be able to take care of you.

It is normal to see your surviving parent cry, be sad, and not be themselves, especially in the beginning. If you see signs that your parent's grief is intensifying over time and notice evidence of excessive drinking, sleeping all day, frequent, uncontrollable sobbing or that they are unable to take care of themselves, you, or your siblings, they may be in need of professional help. Basically, if the person you know your parent to be seems to have disappeared, this could be a sign of depression or other serious problems. Trust your gut to tell you if something's not right. If you are unsure, check it out with an adult close to you or your family. Remember, it is not your job to fix your parent. They need to help themselves.

If your parents were divorced, you may be feeling another kind of change, as 14-year-old Katie, who lost her dad in the attack on the World Trade Center, explains:

> *I've always been really close to Mom, but some things have changed. She and my dad were divorced, so I'd spend half my time living with her and half with him. Now I'm with her 24/7, and I like that, but we sometimes both get annoyed and need some space.*

Mary's parents were also divorced before her father died. He had remarried, though, which means there is another person in the picture for Mary — her stepmother.

> *My parents had been divorced for many years before my dad died, and I think that made it so that my relationship with my mom didn't really change that much overall. My dad remarried before he got sick and died. I still keep in contact with my stepmother. Our relationship has definitely changed. I don't see her very often, and when I do, my dad is always on our minds. He was the only connection*

between us and now he is gone. We always say little things
about my dad when we are together. My stepmother just got
remarried recently, and that is a little weird. I am unsure
of where our relationship is going from here.

Remarriage is challenging, and it brings up a lot of conflicting emotions: Do you like this person? How do your siblings feel? Does your surviving parent seem happier? Will you move? Remarriage also brings up two bigger questions: What role is the stepparent going to try to take in your life? What happens now to the memory of your loved one?

It's hard to accept a new adult in your life. Hopefully, your surviving parent is talking openly with you about the situation and what it means for your family. It's okay if it hurts at first to see your surviving parent happy again with someone else. On the one hand, having two adults in your household can make you appear like a more "normal" family to the outside world. On the other hand, having a relationship with your stepparent — and even liking them — may make you feel disloyal to the parent who died.

If your surviving parent is seriously dating or planning to remarry, you might be questioning how he or she can love the new person, yet still love the parent you lost. Here is the way I look at it: Have you ever had two close — even best — friends at the same time? You love them both but for different reasons. Or perhaps you've had two boyfriends or girlfriends (preferably at different times!). When you look back on those relationships, the feelings, intensity, and memories of each are as different as they are special. You had room in your heart for both people and your feelings for one don't lessen the feelings for the other.

Stepparents, when they get it right, can find a place in your heart and in your life that does nothing to diminish the place you have for your parent who died. When they get it wrong or are threatened by the memory of your loved one and remove all traces of them (photos, knickknacks, et cetera) and don't allow you to speak about them, they can cause a lot of damage. If this happens to you, it's so important to communicate with your surviving parent, either in private or by writing them a note, telling them what you see and how you are feeling. If you don't get anywhere, go to another trusted adult (teacher, best friend's parent, coach) who will listen to you.

You and your parent may not find all the answers at first; it's a situation that takes some getting used to. Give it time.

Thinking of your parent alone, without a partner, can also be upsetting. Casey values her relationship with her mother, but she also worries about the future:

Me and my mom are all that the other has now.
Sometimes that makes us really close, but at other times
it's really difficult to live with. I love my mom so much,
and I'm so thankful for everything that she has done for
me. I can't imagine raising a child on my own. But it
also means that we only have each other, so when we are
fighting, it's really hard because I have no one to talk to.
I'm really worried about what will happen to my mom
when I go away to college. The thought of her living all
alone terrifies me.

It's natural to worry about how your parent will handle his or her empty "nest" alone. But notice that Casey talks about *when*, not *if*, she goes to college. No matter how well you take care of your surviving parent, you're still a teenager, and you need time and space not only to grieve but also to live. Your life after loss still includes friends, school, sports, college, and more. If you start to feel your surviving parent's needs are too much for you to handle, find someone who will listen. Another trusted adult may be able to talk to your parent for you.

Sometimes the different terms of a relationship with a surviving parent are overwhelming. At 16, three years after losing her father, Ella observes her family life is totally changed:

Unfortunately, my relationships with my sister and my mother deteriorated rapidly after 9/11. I think we all got so hurt, we forgot how to really be there for each other. To escape from the craziness of my house I decided to go to boarding school. It's hard being away from everyone, but I think in the long run, it will be better for my family without the daily clashes we used to experience.

Ella made a tough choice but did what felt best to her. Would Ella still be home if her father were alive? Probably, but it's actually tough to predict. As I wrote in my story, my older brother was clashing with my parents before they died, and I doubt that the situation would have changed much had our family stayed intact. If you're feeling ripped off because your family has changed drastically, you're not alone. You didn't ask for this to happen — and it stinks. Yes, grief and pain can bring you closer to those you love, but as in Ella's case, loss can also shatter family bonds.

The bond between you and your surviving parent isn't the only one that is different now. If you have brothers and sisters, your bond has likely changed with them too. You may find yourself stepping into your deceased parent's shoes for certain roles. As I wrote in my story, in some ways I became a surrogate mom for my youngest brother, who needed me to provide a structure for our home life as it unraveled after my mother's death and especially after my father died. If you're a girl who has lost your mom, it's not unusual for your siblings to rely on you for "mom" things, like cooking meals, cleaning, doing laundry, or comforting them when they're upset.

If you're a guy who has lost your dad, you might be expected by your younger brothers and sisters to handle the "dad" things, like yardwork and small repairs around the house.

Eighteen-year-old Abbey H., whose mother died when she was 14 (her younger sister and brother were 6 and 8), shares her story:

> *My role as an older sibling jumped to one of being a responsible caretaker. In the first six months to a year after my mom's death, I stayed with my siblings whenever my dad needed to get out of the house. It was hard because I was used to Mom always being there to watch them, and I pretty much just looked out for myself. Then again, I didn't have my driver's license yet, so I didn't have that much of a choice. I already knew how to do my own laundry and clean. I had been helping Mom with those chores since the arrival of my two siblings, so that wasn't as much of a problem. As I watch them grow up, I feel a need to be their protector and nurturer,*

to baby them and look out for them. Sometimes I get
frustrated with this role I've been playing, and when my
dad disciplines them, I don't try to jump in and take up
for them. It's weird being 18 and acting like I'm 38
sometimes. I constantly worry about what will happen to
them once I leave for college, especially my younger sister,
who is at an age when she needs someone to nurture her.

While some readjustment of responsibilities is part of your new reality, it isn't your job to become a surrogate mom or dad. If you feel that a new family role is putting too much pressure on you, talk to your parent or another trusted adult.

You might simply feel you should be "strong" — the "man" or the "woman" of the house. Being there for your brothers and sisters is great. But being there and being "strong" at the expense of allowing yourself to grieve isn't going to help your siblings or you through your grief.

Caitlin, 13, whose father died of cancer when she was 7, expresses what many teens say really stinks about how loss affects life and family:

You might have to semi-replace your loved one (clean, do
laundry, take care of brothers or sisters). You are forced
to grow up faster than you thought, and sometimes you

*can't handle it. Just do what I do: go crying to Mommy
or Daddy. It helps so much!*

The best thing you can do for yourself and your family is
to be open to your own grief process as well as that of your
siblings.

Grief brings on intense feelings, and sometimes these can
be difficult to talk about. Our Healing Circle leader Ed
Whitacre points out that sometimes teens don't want to
"burden" other family members by talking about their feelings. If you're wondering where to go with your intense
feelings of grief, then remember what Hilary said earlier, and
try turning to the person who's "got your back" — your surviving parent. Addressing your feelings by talking to your
parent helps you and sets a good example for your younger
siblings.

When I asked CZC campers how their relationships had
changed with their siblings, the responses were mixed. Some,
like sisters Elizabeth and Emily S., feel closer but also more
protective of their younger siblings:

> *I look after [my youngest sister] a lot more than I
> usually would, and I tell her I love her a lot. Emily and
> I just get along better in general — we used to fight a lot
> more than we do now.*   — Elizabeth

I appreciate my sisters more since our loss, and I feel obligated to protect my [younger] sister. We still fight, but they know I love them. — Emily S.

That protective feeling might also extend to your parent. I've heard often at camp that kids don't want to make things more difficult for their surviving parent, so they make a sort of pact with their siblings to chill out when it comes to fighting and arguments. Matt's sister Amy was 11 when their mother died. When asked to describe their relationships with each other, Matt and Amy's responses are almost identical. Matt says about Amy, "As we get older, we don't talk about Mom as much, but I can tell that we have gotten closer over time. We don't fight as much and try to be more of a help to my dad." And Amy says about Matt, "My brother and I have gotten closer, and we don't fight as much because we don't want to make my dad upset." Like many other CZC campers I've met, Matt and Amy have seen their surviving parent dealing with so much "stuff," they don't want to cause them more by fighting. If you sense your parent is stressed, it will be a big help to them if you don't sweat the small stuff with your brothers and sisters. You may simply find that the things you and your siblings argued about in the past aren't such a big deal anymore.

How your relationship with your brothers and sisters changes after loss can have a lot to do with the age range

among you. Emily F. has found that being the oldest means
her feelings are very different from her siblings':

> *I'm the oldest, and the next one is four years younger*
> *than me. Most of my siblings were just about too young*
> *to grieve like I was and feel the way I was feeling. In*
> *a way, it pulled us apart. I felt so much older than all*
> *of them.*

Abbey H., who is also several years older than her siblings,
adds this:

> *My siblings were confused about the concept of the finality*
> *of her death because they were at such a young age. My*
> *sister was 6, in first grade, and my brother was 8, in second*
> *grade. Death was intangible and unclear to them. For them*
> *it was as if she was on an extended vacation or business*
> *trip . . . except it was an eternal trip, and she wasn't*
> *coming back. I do remember, though, when my dad came*
> *home from the hospital to tell us she had passed on, my sister*
> *screamed and screamed. She at least understood something*
> *very scary had happened. At 14, I of course understood*
> *what death was and the idea that my mom was never*
> *coming back. As we all have grown older in the past four*

*years, they understand she won't be coming back and I have
better accepted the fact that I am a motherless child.*

Mary isn't the oldest, but she is beginning to understand
how the years between her and her older sister have made it
more difficult to connect after losing their dad:

> *My sister went off to college shortly after my dad died. I
> think that prevented us from really talking about my dad.
> We are also about six years apart, so I think it was hard
> for her as a senior in high school to talk with me as a sixth
> grader. We were kind of on different levels. Now I've grown
> up more and we are on closer levels, but she lives [far
> away], so it is hard to have a good chance to talk about our
> dad. When we do see each other face-to-face, there tend to be
> other things that we would rather talk about.*

Peter talks about his lack of a relationship with his sister:

> *My sister and I have never been close. Before my dad died,
> we were always fighting and never talked. After my dad
> died, it kind of stayed that way. We don't fight anymore,
> but we still never talk. Sometimes I wonder if she really
> is my sister — sometimes she seems like more of a cousin.*

Casey's half brother is 29 and doesn't live nearby. She would like an opportunity to bond with him but is unsure that will happen:

> In the last couple of years, we have sort of lost touch. I wish that we were closer, because he is the only other one who knew my dad in the way that I did — as a dad. Just having me and my mom at home can be really difficult, because when we have a bad day, we only have each other to take it out on.

Melissa's relationships with her two sisters bond them in mostly unspoken ways:

> I keep in touch with my older sister mostly by phone. We have a positive relationship, but it's distant. With my younger sister, I also have a positive relationship. We don't really talk about Mom or what happened. We have a lot of different opinions about the past. It makes me really tense to talk about my mom, and I think it's that way for her too. We do seem to understand that it is really different without our mother here and that we have to stick together.

Relationships with your siblings can become awkward or uncomfortable as roles change and need to be filled. My brothers (both older and younger) at different points both described me as their mother, sister, and best friend. When they started dating, they compared all the girls they were dating to me, from height, to athletic ability, to eye color. My response to that was "Gross! Are you trying to date me?" I didn't want the pressure of being their mother or their best friend or female role model. I just wanted to be their sister. It wasn't that I was extra nurturing or motherly toward them. I was just there and was consistent and was someone female to check in with. It was a role I assumed but never was comfortable with.

Every family is different. The years between Cassie and her older half brother — as well as other issues that Cassie can only guess about — have severed rather than strengthened their bond:

> *The relationship between me and my brother changed immensely. My brother is twelve years older than me and he was 26 when my dad passed away. I'm not sure what the reason is, I can only speculate, but he abandoned me. I haven't talked to him since two weeks after my dad's funeral. The only contact I've had with him was a card on my 15th birthday and a graduation card that he signed. It's hard because I needed my brother to be there for me, and he wasn't. It was like I lost two people when my dad died. I think it was because he couldn't handle the fact that*

my dad died. I was too big of a reminder of my dad for
him. But it still hurts, and I still miss him.

Like Cassie, you may miss a sibling who is shutting you out. As painful as this is, try to remember that your brothers and sisters are also hurting. You may feel so vulnerable and raw that you'll hesitate to risk loving and losing anyone again. It's natural to feel this way after a parent dies, but remember, as Healing Circle leader Kurt Stiefvater says, "Loving others is a risk worth taking." You may even find you have a new sense of caring and compassion for your family.

If you are an only child, 14-year-old Brittany sums up what could be your feelings too:

I don't have any siblings, but at a time like this, I'd like
to have one.

On top of everything else going on after a parent dies, dealing with the changing relationships in your family is tough. It's hard enough just missing your parent who died. Things have changed not only because of your parent's absence from the house, but also because of the hole they left within the family. A family role is now vacant. The mere fact that there is one person fewer in the family means everything is going to shift. The changes your surviving parent must deal with forces your relationship with them to change, and your siblings are trying to adapt and readjust just like you are. From dentist appointments to mowing the lawn to coaching soccer to holiday traditions, the many roles your deceased parent played are either being reassigned to the remaining members of the family or are being left undone, causing everything from minor to major disruptions within your family unit. Healing Circle leader Jill FitzGerald urges teens not to be afraid to "wave a red flag" to let your family know what you need or when you are feeling overwhelmed. Remember that it takes a lot of courage and cooperation to get through this together.

7

How Others React to Your Loss

*The hardest thing about my loss is the way people
never know how to act and usually
say something painful or stupid.*

Has this happened to you yet? You're with a new group of people,
and somehow the subject of parents comes up. It might be
because it's almost Father's Day or Mother's Day, you're spending
the night at a friend's house and meeting their parents for the first
time, or there's a carpooling schedule to work out. Then there's
the moment when you know you have to tell people about your
loss. How do you say it? What words do you use? How do
people react? And most of all, how do you wish they'd react?

I remember the stunned silence again and again when I met
a new person — a friend's parents, new teacher, or coach —
and somewhere along the line, my mom or dad came up.
"What do your parents do?" or "Can your mom give you a ride
over?" or "What did you get your dad for Father's Day?" people might ask. When this happens, do you find yourself in the
position of making a split-second decision? "Do I feel like
investing the energy to tell this person?" "Do I feel like dealing

with the big *silence* after they find out and then watching them become frozen and speechless?" I remember patting kids and adults on the back after they found out my parents died. I could see their own mortality wheel spinning, and I would tell them, "It's okay. I'm not going to fall apart." It's ironic, isn't it, when somehow your loss becomes all about them.

I can also remember kids intentionally trying to hurt me by saying something about my parents. I vividly remember playing dodgeball in the fourth grade — I caught the ball and got this kid in my class out. He yelled at me, "Hey, Barribeau [my maiden name], I'm glad your mom died." Nice kid, huh?

It's difficult to tell people about your loss, right after or even years later. One of our adult CZC volunteers confessed to me that more than thirty years after losing her dad in a car accident when she was 12, she still feels her cheeks flush and heart pound when she has to tell someone new about her loss.

When I asked the teens I interviewed for this book how people react when they learn about their parent's death, many described a similar silence or awkwardness. This isn't surprising; most people, especially kids your own age, aren't comfortable talking about death. Most teens around you will have little or no personal experience with death. Healing Circle leader Kurt Stiefvater says, "For today's youth, it seems more like death is something that only happens to people on the news or really old people who have lived a long life. When they hear of the death of someone related to a friend, they are caught off guard and don't know what to say."

How many of the following stories ring true for you?

Emily L., who lost her dad to cancer when she was 15, describes it this way:

> They *get uncomfortable and usually tell me they are sorry. I hate bringing it up, but I hate even more when people don't know. I feel like that event has defined so much of who I am, that I am almost deceiving them by not telling them that he died. I don't blame people for feeling sorry for me. I feel sorry when people tell me they've lost a parent. It's hard even for me to know how to react. I usually try to make it seem like it's not a big deal and change the subject more for their benefit, because I think people usually just don't know what to say.*

You too might relate to Emily's feeling that she has to "make it seem like it's not a big deal" in order to make others feel comfortable. There's no easy way to share this part of your life with others. Not only do you have to handle your own feelings, you often have to field lots of questions and reactions, as Cassie explains:

When the subject of my dad passing away comes up, I find that each person reacts differently. Some people try to be sympathetic. They mean well. They are the ones who say, "Oh, my God, I'm so sorry." Then they continue to ask a whole bunch of questions that I have no desire to answer. I know that might sound mean, and I understand why they apologize, but after a while it seems to me that they are just empty words. To me those apologies are just said because people are uncomfortable and have nothing else to say. I would just rather someone say nothing at all.

Some people know just the right thing to say to make me feel better. Sometimes they talk about an experience that they had with loss, and others talk about a memory that they had of my dad. Other people choose to ignore it when it is mentioned that my dad died. They pretend that nothing was said at all. Sometimes that is the easiest for me, because then I don't have to explain the whole story.

The hardest reaction that I've had to deal with is the one that came from people who didn't know he died. My dad died on Thanksgiving, a major travel holiday. A lot of people were away that weekend and didn't see his obituary. So during the months after, my mom and I constantly ran into people who had no clue that he had died. They would come up to us and ask how he was, and

we would have to break the news that he passed away.
Their reactions varied from shock to sadness. The hardest
reaction was when they would cry. It would make me so
uncomfortable and confused. I wasn't sure if I had to
apologize for making them sad. It also made me want
to cry, but I would just hold it in for fear that it would
upset them even more.

It's been about eight years since Lora's father died of a
stroke, and now that she's in college, telling people about her
loss is starting fresh:

When I came to college, I found a new dilemma: I had to
tell people again. In high school, most of my friends went
to elementary school with me and knew me when my dad
died, and those who hadn't known me learned from those
who did. The few times I did have to tell people in middle
and high school, they would tend to say something to the
effect of, "Oh, I'm sorry," and then nervously change the
topic. When I came to college, I was completely afraid of
that happening again. I found that as "almost adults,"
people are more open to the idea of talking to you. I try to
wait until it comes up in conversation, like if they see a
picture of my dad on my desk or see me wearing a CZC

T-shirt. When I do tell them, I try to end the statement with something to the effect of, though it has been very difficult, I have been incredibly blessed in other ways since then that probably would have never happened if my dad hadn't died. People are still really shocked, and you can tell they're searching for the right words to say. That's why I try and carry the conversation from that point, because I know they're afraid of saying something wrong. Sometimes the shock is because they've never had anyone close to them die; other times it is because they have, and they thought they were alone. Most of the time, I feel pressure to act "happier" or "more normal" than usual around them to assure them that I still live my life like anyone else. Sometimes they're shocked because I act so "normal" about it. Sometimes people will ask more questions (either right then or if it comes up again, later), like how or when, and I will tell them in as much detail as they ask. I wait until they press for more details because I don't want to make them any more uncomfortable.

Like Emily L., Cassie, and other CZC teens, Lora expresses concern for the "comfort" of others. Here's what other teens have to say about people's reactions to their loss:

Fourteen-year-old Beth, who lost her father to cancer when she was 8:

> *When I tell people about my dad, they are usually*
> *speechless. They usually can't believe I lost my dad at*
> *such a young age. They usually go through the whole "I am*
> *so sorry" deal.*

Eamon, who was 11 when his father died in the attack on the World Trade Center:

> *Most people usually say, "I'm so sorry to hear about it"*
> *and then try to get off that subject as quickly as humanly*
> *possible.*

Franco, Eamon's older brother:

> *Some people have gotten teary-eyed and hugged me; many*
> *have told me they had no idea and that they were sorry*
> *for me.*

Hilary, whose father also died on 9/11:

> *Most of the time people are in shock for a minute or*
> *two, like they can't believe what they're hearing. They*

*eventually express how sorry they are, and quickly
walk away.*

Melissa, whose mother died of a drug overdose:

*When my mother died, I didn't have friends who leaped
up and tried to comfort me. I felt alone. I could hear
people whisper about me and say things that really hurt.
I was desperate for someone to talk to. I would force
myself not to let my emotions come out; I wouldn't cry
or even frown. I would always wear a mask. It still is
hard to cry in front of my peers because they don't know
how it feels and that makes it all the harder.*

Suzanne is 16. She was 8 when her dad died of cancer:

*There are mixed reactions, and normally I don't tell
everyone I meet. My closest friends know, but I try not to
make a big deal out of it because I don't like being
different. I've experienced in the past that sometimes
when I've told someone that my dad died, they've treated
me either like I'm glass or like I need extra attention, or
else they try and avoid me. I don't want to be treated any
differently because of the fact that my dad died, because
that doesn't change who I am.*

Matt, who was 14 when his mom died:

People say "Oh, I am so sorry." Yeah, I'm sure they are . . .
and it's nice of them to say . . . but I really don't get
into it with most people — just those who are close to me.

Hannah, who was 9 when her father died after a long battle with cancer:

People give me the silent treatment. They don't really
know what to say other than "I'm sorry," but I don't
blame them for it. How would anyone know what to say?
I don't take it personally when that happens because that
is an awkward situation in which to be.

Kurt Stiefvater and our other Healing Circle leaders hear stories like these at camp and in their private practices. One thing that becomes easier to understand when teens discuss people's reactions at camp is that the words "I'm sorry" don't always indicate an apology or even pity. Those words "can be offered as an expression of empathy, sorrow, and compassion," Kurt points out. "So, 'I'm sorry' can mean 'I feel sorrow' as well as 'I feel regret.'"

An issue we discuss in Healing Circles is how to let people know what you are and are not comfortable talking about. As so many teens expressed above, you might find yourself taking care of others when discussing your loss. It's not always easy to let others know what you're feeling, but if you practice, you'll find you get better and better at it. As Kurt says, "When people are helpful and understanding, let them know that you appreciate their support or willingness to listen. When people say things that annoy or upset you, find ways to tell them how they might be more helpful to you at that particular time. If you are not really capable of giving feedback at that time, consider simply telling the other person that you don't want to talk about it right now and that another time might be better. Perhaps after some reflection you can share more or let the person know what comments bothered you."

Wouldn't it be great if there was a cheat sheet that listed the "right" things to say to someone who is grieving? Here's how teens who shared the feelings above say *they wish* others would react:

> *I wish they didn't have to react to me. I wish I never had*
> *to tell anyone that he died and that they would just know.*
> *There really is no good way to react, but I suppose if I*
> *had to tell someone, I would want them to not be afraid*
> *to ask me questions about it. I'd rather them have the*
> *whole story than just know that he died and that be it.*
>
> — Emily L.

I'm not sure about how I wish they would react. I think it depends on the way I'm feeling. Sometimes I wish people would just leave it be. I don't need apologies because it wasn't their fault. I hate feeling abnormal, and having someone focus on the fact that my dad died makes me feel like I'm not normal at all. Other times it's nice to have someone express the fact that they are there for me if I ever need to talk. It makes me feel like someone cares enough about me to listen. — Cassie

I guess I wish people would see it as more normal. I remember mentally taking a step backward one time and looking at my life in an objective way, and it shocked me. It doesn't seem that strange to me that I saw my dad practically dead on our living room floor because I've lived with it for almost ten years now, and that memory is a part of my life. Other people see it as a huge oddity, which I guess in our society it is. From people's reactions, it almost seems as though it is more expected and acceptable to have a parent walk out on you than to die in front of you. I wish they would understand that, yes, my dad being gone is something I live with every day, but it's not something that keeps me, in a deep, dark depression 24/7. Yes, I remember that morning every day, but it's normal for me, and I live my life like anyone else. A lot of people react by thinking that they can't say certain words or phrases around me or that they need to be careful because I'm "fragile." I wish that they would understand that, yeah, I may have certain buttons that can be pushed, but we all do — mine are just different. It's okay to act normal around me (and usually people do after a while of getting to know me), and you don't need to try to protect me from getting hurt again. A guest speaker in one of my nursing classes put it like this: I don't care so much what you say, as long as I know you care. — Lora

I'm fine with the way they react because I know that's how I would react if I was talking to someone in that situation. — Eamon

I don't wish they would react any way because I have become accustomed to people's reactions to me telling them of my father's death and therefore do not care.
— Franco

I wish people would react just naturally and not let it bother them, because it doesn't change who I am. I'm still the same person; I'm just missing a part of my life that they have. — Suzanne

119

I honestly don't know . . . I think the fact that they are just there for me and will listen when I need them to is enough. — Matt

I wish they would not be afraid to ask about it. It is okay to ask! I won't go into hysterics if you ask about it! It actually feels good to talk about it. — Hannah

And 13-year-old Erin, who was 6 when her father died of cancer, adds:

If they haven't experienced it, then they shouldn't say that they understand when they really don't.

Healing Circle leader Ed Whitacre agrees with Kurt that we learn to be uncomfortable with death in our society, and it's only natural that we want to help people avoid or minimize pain. "But the more comfortable we are about talking about the loss, the person who died, who he or she was, what we miss, loved, hated, our own feelings, etcetera, then the more comfortable others can be talking about it with us, because they see we can handle the feelings and they don't have to protect us," Ed explains.

Try letting people know how you feel when it comes to

talking about your loss. As Ed says, "Some folks may never be comfortable talking about the loss with you because they are protecting themselves." You may have to accept that some people don't give you the reaction you long for. But you can practice letting others know how you feel and how much or how little you want to discuss your loss. It takes a lot of courage to deal with other people's reactions to what happened to you. Finding others who share your experience can help a lot. And if you're lucky enough to have friends who are willing to listen even if they haven't walked in your shoes, you'll feel more supported.

What do you experience when it comes to talking to your friends? Casey points out what helps — and what doesn't:

> *I have a few friends who I can talk to most of the time. Mostly they just help by letting me talk, rather than actually saying anything that helps me. I don't care that they don't know what to say, because I understand that they must feel really uncomfortable. I just appreciate that they will listen when I need them to. The only thing that does bother me is when people who have divorced parents tell me they understand because their dad doesn't live with them.*

Hannah appreciates the support of her closest friends:

I can talk to my very close friends, because I know that if I am having a hard time dealing with my father's death, they won't mind sitting and listening to me vent and will lend me a shoulder to cry on. There are very few people that I will talk to about my loss, because I feel like I'm bombarding them with my problems. However, when you find those few friends who you feel comfortable talking with, you don't feel that way at all because you know you would do the same for them.

Nineteen-year-old Abby O., who lost her mom at age 14, also welcomes her friends' reaching out:

I have found that kids who have not experienced the death of a loved one aren't necessarily scared to talk about your loss with you. Over the years, I have come to find that my friends do want to know about my mom's death, but more importantly, about her life. Most of my best friends, especially now that I am in college, never got the chance to meet her, but that doesn't mean I can't talk about her. People may seem scared, but they are also compassionate, and even if they don't know what to say in response, it is okay to talk to them about what has happened to you.

Lora chooses to talk about her loss with others who "get it":

*I have two types of friends, regular friends and CZC
friends. I don't really talk to my regular friends about my
dad's death, and rarely about my dad in general. Why?
Because I get the sense that it makes them uncomfortable. I
can't give a specific example, but often when I mention my
dad, even in a passing comment, I get the "sympathetic look"
or some other sympathetic comment. And I know that they're
just trying to understand, and it's not their fault that they
can't. But sometimes all I need is for someone to laugh along
with me at a story of something funny my dad did or for
them to just continue the conversation like normal. This is
the main reason I never directly discuss my dad's actual
death with people unless they ask, because they'll try and say
something that they think will make the situation better, and
they can't. A lot of people say, "Well, he's in a better place
now." I know that. That's the problem. He's gone. He's no
longer here. I know it's selfish, but I want him here. They
won't say what I'm looking for — which is something my
camp friends know. They know that maybe I don't need
them to say anything. Maybe I need them to say something
I've brought up before and am overlooking in the heat of the
moment. Maybe I need them to share their experience with
me. Whatever it is, they know.*

Sixteen-year-old Suzanne has a hopeful story to share of the way a friend has been there for her:

Most of my friends know that my dad died when I was in elementary school, and that I only live with my mom. But, really, I have only talked to one person about it. I could not have asked for a better way for the guy who I shared with to take it. But there is a bit of a story to go with this. I had met Charles about a month before Easter, and he had been over to my house and seen the pictures we have of my dad around, and while he knew that I would tell him in due time, he never pushed me into telling him. When I finally did, he didn't even say anything, he just wrapped me up in a hug and told me that he would always be there for me. That really meant a lot. On Easter Sunday, my mom and I planned on going to where my dad is buried. Charles came and helped us put the flowers on the grave, and we just all stood there and talked for a while. On the way back to the house, I completely opened up to him and talked about my dad, about camp, and about how both have impacted my life. He just simply listened, assuring me that if I didn't feel comfortable telling him, I didn't need to. I think that was one of the best ways to talk to a friend; just let it come when you feel like you can trust the person you are sharing with.

Suzanne is lucky to have found such an understanding friend in Charles. If you can find friends you can trust, it may feel easier to let them know what's going on with you. Franco has also found a friend who isn't afraid to ask about his dad:

I can talk to my friends about my father because they understand that I'm not uncomfortable with it. They sometimes ask questions about him, but it never changes the mood of the conversation. One of my friends has asked on more than one occasion how I feel talking about my dad, and I've told him I am proud and comfortable with talking about him. He is very sensitive when we get on the subject, and I respect him for being very sincere about it.

Matt has also found that talking to trusted friends helps:

There are a few friends I feel I can talk to, and I do. Usually I talk and they listen, and I do the same for them. The conversations consist of me going on and on about my mom — how much I miss her — and they just listen. That's all I really need. Someone to listen.

Give yourself permission to tell as little or as much as you want to about having lost a loved one. You may feel a little guilty if you decide not to divulge your loss to everyone who asks. It doesn't minimize your feelings toward your parent who died, it just means you don't feel like going "into it" at that particular moment or with that particular person. I have responded to questions such as, "What does your father do?" by answering "Sales." My father was in sales, and I'm not lying, I'm just not expounding the answer. We've all gotten the phone call "Is your mother/father there?" You can answer no if you feel like it because, again, that is technically true. I have had kids tell me that they have told people on the phone, "No, they are dead," when solicitors call. They *never* call back once you tell them that! They can't wait to get off the phone!

I have found there are two types of people: those who "Get It" and those "Who Don't." I always had a hard time being around people who didn't "get it" because they either weren't *real* to me or I just couldn't interact with them for long because I didn't have the patience. If you can, be patient and understanding with those who don't get it. They are just in a completely different place and are not encouraged by society to talk about death or feelings associated with death. And they certainly don't want to be reminded it could happen to them.

And, when you find the people who get it, exhale, relax . . . and be yourself. They will understand when you want to be quiet, when you want to cry, and when you just want a hug. They will be true gifts to you.

8

REMEMBERING OUR LOVED ONES

Somehow, I know you are watching.

Even though they are no longer here, we will always be connected to the loved ones we've lost. When you do well on a test or sing a solo in choir or hit a home run in the last inning of the game, do you ever imagine your parent's reaction? Can you picture their smile, or hear their words of praise? You might feel as if your mom or dad is standing right next to you.

Moments like these are often bittersweet — you feel happy for your accomplishment but sad your parent is not there to share it with you. It's tough to have birthdays, graduation, and other big events without your mom or dad. So, how can you keep your parent in your life and stay connected with them? There are no magic secrets to doing this; you have to decide what works for you. And what works for you can change over time. Writing in your journal, for instance, may be a huge help in feeling connected, but it might not feel the same to you a few months or years later, and you'll need to explore other ideas.

Finding ways to stay connected to those we've lost is a big

part of the journey. It may not always be easy but it's something important to do no matter what the circumstances of our losses were. Here are some ideas you may relate to:

I look at the stars to stay connected. To me, my dad is just right above them. So the stars are just a way I often "talk" to him — if it is a starry night — because I feel like he can hear me. — Suzanne

I pray a lot. Something that my dad and I had in common that the rest of our house didn't really was our deep faith in God. The rest of my family believes in God, but my dad and I were especially devout. Praying is sort of my way of honoring what he taught me about God and religion and faith. I think about him, I talk about him, and these things in themselves help me stay connected. Sometimes when I'm doing something I'm proud of, I'll pretend that he's there. I'll picture him standing somewhere, just watching me and smiling. I'll think about what he might have said to me if he really could be there. — Elizabeth

I sing, I try to be happy, I laugh, and I live. Even though I fail horribly, I try to appreciate everyone and everything

and not let life's little issues get me down. I know that he would be proud of all I have and will accomplish.

— Ella

I go to his alma mater, which is a pretty big connection. I keep in touch with his side of the family. I look at pictures, and we still have a lot of his stuff at our house (books, albums, etc.). I'm even living in a house next year owned by his best friends from college. We used to visit the house in the summer, so it has lots of memories in it.

— Emily L.

I wear some of his old jackets and look at pics.

— Caitlin

I listen to the same music and watch the same movies that he did. I continue the traditions that he and I had.

— Brittany

At night sometimes, I talk to my dad in heaven, and I know he is listening. I also like to go through photo albums and watch family movies of the good old days. Doing that helps me remember my dad clearly, and it brings back some warm, fuzzy memories.   — Hilary

I occasionally talk as if I'm talking to him. — Eamon

I keep his memory alive by thinking and talking about him often. I keep my dad's picture on my desk. It's really nice for me to look at it and think about my dad. Sometimes I have something that I really want to tell him, so I might say it to the picture instead. Also, when I wish he was here to talk to, I write a letter to him telling him everything that is on my mind. — Mary

When my mom and I are at the beach on the day my dad died, we put two roses in the ocean to kind of say, "We miss you, but we're doing okay." — Erin

I do lots of things to stay connected to my dad. Over the past few years, I've accumulated many things that make me feel he's around me. I carry around the last picture he and I took together. I had it with me the day I got my license, the day I graduated, and my first day of college. I wear his wedding ring on my right middle finger. I have been wearing it since the day he passed away. My mom gave it to me, and I keep it on — it makes me feel like I have a piece of him with me each day. I write a lot. My dad used to love reading what I wrote, and he would always encourage me to write more. I like to go to the cemetery sometimes and read to him. I talk to him every night, not out loud but in my head. Just to let him know how everything is going. It was hard for me at first, because I felt like I was talking to air, but then it began to help because I know he's up there listening to me. — Cassie

On birthdays and anniversaries, I ride my horse out to the place where we buried some of his ashes and go and talk to him. I also release balloons with messages. Another way is through camp: Every time that I go, I feel like I'm connecting with him and honoring him and remembering. — Casey

Every Thanksgiving, my dad's family all gets together and gives each other ornaments for the Christmas tree. Ever since his death, we've gotten a star for my dad. We now have three stars. — Emily F.

Holidays and other big days can be a thoughtful time of reflection too:

I'm just pretty quiet around special days. — Peter

If your relationship with your parent was troubled before he or she died, staying connected can be especially challenging.

Melissa's mother died of a drug overdose, and made some choices Melissa knows she doesn't want to repeat:

> *In order to stay connected to my mom, I have a picture of her hanging in my room. I also have the glass cross that she gave me when I was really little and in foster care. I use my voice and sing. I stay strong. I saw my mother as a weak person. She didn't have much control over her own life. She was always clinging to some guy and relying on someone else to take care of her. I stay connected with her by doing the opposite. I am not ever going to rely on other people to pay for my food and take care of me. I can take care of myself. I want to be an independent and strong person. So I strive to change the patterns of my past. . . . I want to make a difference in my world for the good.*

Not all parents are good parents and not all memories are pleasant. If you were in a situation where there was physical, emotional, or substance abuse, the last thing you are going to want to do is revisit those memories. People often idealize or put the person who died on a pedestal and make them out to be a perfect person. This is extremely difficult to cope with when the person you lived with was not a good or nice person.

Jesse is 17; she was 12 when her father, who had been abusive, died of cancer:

I generally try to forget about him, though I write an occasional angry poem. — Jesse

Another challenge can be that your parent died when you were very young or not even born yet, and you don't have any memories at all. Jason was 2 when his dad died from a heart attack. When he came to camp at age 15, he was grieving as much if not more than some of the kids who had experienced a more recent loss. He was in a lot of pain and was angry at the kids who had their parents longer than he did. He felt "ripped off." His mother never told him any stories about his dad, and he doesn't know anyone who knew his dad. He doesn't have anyone to offer connections to his dad, to help him understand who his dad was as a person or whether they have any similarities.

Videos, tape recordings, and photographs are treasures. If your family is moving or making other changes after your loss, be sure you hang onto these. Even if they feel too painful to look at or listen to now, I guarantee there will come a time when you will thank yourself for keeping these precious memories safe and in good condition.

I've met many kids who have made memory boxes for photos, videos, letters, poems, and other mementos. A scrapbook is also a good way to record memories, using photos, poetry, and collage. You might want to divide your scrapbook into two parts: your life with your parent in it and your life now.

Fifteen-year-old Emily F. has found comfort in compiling a scrapbook:

> *One of my biggest fears after my dad died was that I would start to forget about him, so I made a big scrapbook of his life, wrote in a journal all my memories of him, and collected stuff that reminds me of him and put it into a crate. This way, if I ever begin to forget, I can go through these things and remember.*

Holidays and birthdays can bring grief back in waves. Your birthday, Father's Day, Mother's Day, Thanksgiving — these are all "family" times that may never feel quite the same again after your loss. You can't turn back time, but you can create special new traditions that honor your loved one and comfort you as well.

One of the most healing activities we do at camp is a balloon release. You can write a note to your loved one, attach it to a helium-filled balloon, and then let it float up into the sky. Whether you release one balloon or gather with family and friends to release dozens of balloons, the sight of balloons climbing up to the heavens can be very comforting and peaceful.

It's been almost seven years since Hannah's dad died. She and her family have found a special way of using balloons to remember him:

> My father's favorite type of candy was SweeTarts. So on his birthday, my mother, brother, and I blow up balloons with SweeTarts inside and let them float toward heaven, hoping he will receive them.

Lighting candles is a calming ritual during the holidays, on birthdays, or whenever you need to feel peaceful. Matt's neighbors join in remembering his mom at the holidays with candles:

> People in our neighborhood light a blue candle in a window in their home at Christmas, a tradition started by one of our close neighbors. Over the years, fewer houses still do this, but we do and so do some of our neighbors. It's a cool way to remember my mom during her favorite season.

Christmas and Hanukkah can be especially difficult holidays when you've lost a parent. In addition to lighting candles, you and your family can write letters to your loved one to be put in a special stocking or box each year, which can even be shared aloud. Talking about your loved one and your own feelings of grief is especially helpful during the holidays. Share your favorite memories of your loved one at each holiday — your favorite Christmas memory, Thanksgiving memory, and so on.

Graduation is a milestone that can really make you miss your loved one. Try putting a picture of your parent inside your hat or carry a special keepsake in your hand. Many teens also talk about their future weddings and how difficult it will be not to have their parent there. Think about putting a rose or a photo on the altar. Light a candle just for them. Read from a favorite book or play music you know they liked.

Go to the cemetery if you wish. Prepare and share your loved one's favorite food. Make them a card. Nothing is silly or weird. It is all about what it means to you. Here are some other ideas:

On Valentine's Day, my father would always send my mom and me flowers, so every Valentine's Day I send my mom flowers. We always have a special mass said on my dad's birthday and on September 11. — Hilary

We set off fireworks for his birthday, just like huge candles.
— Caitlin

I usually visit her gravesite or get in my car and drive by it and then drive around and go by all the places we used to go together: the barn where our family kept our horses; our favorite restaurants; the state department (where she used to work); favorite stores; our church. — Abby O.

This past year on my dad's birthday, I bought a red balloon and wrote a message to him on it and then found a private place outside and released it into the heavens. — Mary

I made my dad this slide show; it's about five or six songs long. It is of his life, and of him and me, from when I was a baby to our last picture together. And every Thanksgiving Day, which is the day he passed away, I go to the cemetery with my laptop, and I play it for him. Every holiday, my mom and I visit the cemetery. And on each special day, I bring something different to leave there. Sometimes it is a letter I have written him, and other times it is a poem that I have written him or flowers or something that he would have loved. It makes me feel better when I have something to leave there. I've made stepping stones at camp, and I've brought them both to the cemetery at special times. One was on his birthday and the other was on Thanksgiving Day. — Cassie

I sometimes put a notice in the paper for her birthday
and holidays and special occasions. — **Abbey H.**

I threw my father a birthday party when I was in college. My roommates and I got helium balloons and tied them to one of my father's pictures. We got him a cake and ordered Chinese food. My older cousin found out and sent a "Happy Birthday to a Dear Uncle" card. We even sang "Happy Birthday" to him. It made my dad a part of my and my friends' lives. Does that sound crazy? Offbeat? Morbid? Morbidly funny? Good? All of the above? Well, it was what worked for me eight years after he had died — it was what I needed then to still feel connected to him. It was strangely and wonderfully comforting to me.

Another way to stay connected is to find someone who knew your parent and interview them. This is really a great thing to do, especially if you don't have any or many memories of your loved one. Sometimes this is hard, because you have to search out someone who knew them. Do the obvious and ask relatives or friends, teachers, coaches, coworkers . . . just keep digging! Enlist the help of a parent or relative to help you track someone down. See if they will send you a letter or a tape or any photos. Ask them to tell you specific stories. Was your loved one fun? Intellectual? Athletic? Artsy? What were his or her interests? Hopes and dreams? The ones he or she had for you too?

My mother had an older half sister who I never really knew and who lived in a different state. Many years after my mom had died, I wrote her a letter asking her some of these questions. She sent me back a cassette tape that made me cry. She answered all of my questions and more. The most ironic and interesting thing was that the reason that she was my mother's half sister was because her own mother had died when she was three, and her father (my grandfather) was remarried to my grandmother. She related to me on all these levels of mother loss that I never even thought of. She was in her early eighties when she sent me this tape, and she said that her whole life, she felt like an incomplete person due to the loss of her mother.

> *I talk to other family members about her and keep in touch with her closest friends. When learning more about your loved one by talking to their good friends or family members, you may hear stories or learn little tidbits about your loved one that you never knew before.* — Abby O.

Sometimes getting someone to tell you stories will give you important connections to your loved one that you may be missing or are unaware of. This can lead to *huge* steps in your healing. Find people who knew them at different stages of their lives (from childhood, high school, college, single life, early married years, when they first had kids, from clubs or other organizations, or from their workplace). From a parent's previous coworker, for example, you may find out that your mother loved to play cards and practice yoga or that your father liked to play the piano and could speak Latin or that your mom and dad loved to dance. It's an interesting experience — sort of like putting the missing pieces into a puzzle.

When it gets less painful, you may even intentionally revisit your own memories to stay connected. In the beginning, this is hard to fathom. But as the pain eases, you may actually want to sit with those memories and remember. I now do this with a smile on my face and tears in my eyes.

9

WHAT WE WISH PEOPLE HAD TOLD US ABOUT GRIEF

I wish someone had told me there were so many other kids out there dealing with the same thing.

Chances are you've received a lot of advice since your loss — whether you asked for it, or not — about life, death, and grief.

What have *you* learned about grief that *you* wish someone had told *you*?

The teens I interviewed responded to this question with such insight and wisdom. One of my goals for this book was to share stories about loss from the perspectives of *real* teens. Here is their advice straight from the hearts of those who have "been there":

These emotions are normal. Grief is natural. — Philip

It's okay to cry. It doesn't mean you are weak — it means you are strong when you cry. — Suzanne

It's okay to be sad and cry as long as you want to. You don't have to hide it. If other people are uncomfortable because of that, it's their problem. — Casey

I have learned that you will never get over it. You will get better but not fully. I was always told that I would get over it and be fine after a couple of weeks. Well, let me tell you, it may not hit you that a family member died until a couple years after. I didn't actually start grieving until almost five years after my dad passed away.

I will tell you that as life goes on, it is going to be easy at times, but other times it is going to be extremely hard. — Beth

It's okay not to be the strong one. I am the oldest child in my family, and I thought I had to be strong for my dad and sister, but what I really needed was to cry and grieve myself, not be the rock. When I finally was able to have a good cry and look at pictures of my mom, I really benefited. — Matt

You wish they were there with you, even though they're in a better place. You just want that last day, but you know you can't have it. Your loved one may have promised to come back but couldn't overcome the sickness. Many things can happen, and there is nothing you can do about it, and you need to take it slow and think about what is going on. You need to think clearly, so you don't get overwhelmed by the facts.

— Caitlin

[Grief] is so tiring and stressful, you don't even know what to do. Sometimes change is good after losing a loved one. Not everyone knows what to do or say to you, so sometimes they just stare. You will probably lose friends, [but] sometimes friendships just get stronger. These are all the things I wish someone had told me. — Hilary

If only someone had told me that there were so many kids out there dealing with the same thing, it would have made it a little easier. I thought it was like a taboo, losing a parent. I felt like people were saying, "Oooh, look, see that girl: Her dad died, but let's pretend it didn't happen. And since we don't know what to say, let's ignore her and not say anything at all." That was the approach of a lot of kids at my school.

I wish someone had just let me talk. A lot of people had things to say after my dad died, but no one just sat and listened to me. No one let me talk about what I was feeling. I think a lot of people were afraid to let me talk. I don't think they wanted to hear what I had to say. That's why I started to write, as an outlet to get my feelings out.

I wish someone had told me that when someone dies, time doesn't stop. I really thought the world would stop when he died. But I just kept right on going without him here. And when I finally woke up from the haze I was living in, I was amazed to see how much I had missed.

— Cassie

I wish someone had told me to cherish my family while they were all here. As far away as death can seem, anyone could die regardless of age or health. Love your family while you have them!

— Emily F.

My dad died when I was 10, and I have very few memories of him. When he died, many people told me to write down memories of him in a journal. I really wish I had done this, because now, six years later, I can hardly remember him.

— Emily S.

I guess mainly I wish that someone had let me know that I wasn't alone.

— Mary

Elizabeth and Katie offer advice that appears in previous chapters but bears repeating here:

You have to grieve at your own pace in your own way.
Everyone grieves differently. When my dad died, people told
me all these things that I should do — I had journals
coming out my ears — but nobody told me to figure
out what was right for me or what would help me the
most. You can't learn to cope with a loss based on what
other people tell you. You have to do what makes you
happy or what makes you remember or what makes you
feel whole again and go with it without hesitation.

— Elizabeth

I wish that someone had told me it would always be
difficult for me when people first found out about my
dad's death. They never know what to say. I always end
up half comforting them. — Katie

I wish someone had warned me that bad things don't just
happen in adulthood. — Hannah

Kids grieve differently than teens; and teens differently
than adults. No one way is right or wrong. Pretty much
everything you feel is normal and okay. — Lora

It never gets better, just vaguely easier. — Jesse

*I needed the truth. I wish that someone had told me the
reason people were whispering was because they felt
awkward and that they didn't know what to say to me.
Maybe if I had been told that it wasn't my fault sooner,
then I wouldn't still be thinking it was my fault. I felt so
ashamed and dirty, and I thought that I must not be able
to be loved if my mom wanted to kill herself. What I
really needed the most was someone to tell me that I was
not alone. These are just some of the things that I wish
someone had even attempted to explain to me.*

— Melissa

At camp, teens often ask me what *I've* learned about grief.
These are the things that really stand out that I wish someone
had told *me*:

**Grief is something you never get over, and nobody tells
you that.** You are not crazy if you miss having a mom, dad, or
both parents, five, ten, or fifteen years after they've died. It
doesn't mean you can't lead a happy life; it's just something
you have to learn to work with. I view it as an emotional
"handicap" that I deal with every day. Each morning when
I get out of bed, I put on my emotional "braces" and function with them. Sometimes I resent having to put on these

"braces," but most of the time it's automatic and just a part of the routine of my day.

There is a hole inside of you that can never be completely filled. No one will ever love you like your mom or your dad did. Their loss leaves a hole inside you. The trick is to try to fill that hole with bits and pieces of love you get from other people — and with the love and respect you have for yourself. It doesn't ever completely fill the hole, but it makes the hole a lot smaller.

The hole can't be filled by just one person. This is something I learned the hard way. No matter how much you might love a new person in your life, whether they are a mom or dad figure, a boyfriend or girlfriend, or someone you get married to, one person alone can never make up the difference, no matter how much they love you. It is just not possible for someone else to fill that hole entirely. That is just part of the deal.

The point of this book and this chapter in particular is to help you avoid some pain and pitfalls by sharing with you things we wish we'd known but had to learn the hard way. Hopefully, if nothing else, the things you have just read serve as validation that *any* of the things you are feeling and experiencing do not mean you are crazy or not dealing well with your loss. People write "helpful hints" columns on cooking, cleaning, studying for tests, taking tests, and almost anything else you can think of — except dealing with grief. Maybe this chapter can serve as that "list." I was nodding along as I took in these firsthand accounts, even doing a mental checklist along the lines of "Yeah, yeah, got that. Had that one too. No, missed that one, fortunately. Oh, that would have helped me." I hope you nodded and checked a few off your list too.

10

WHAT HELPS

Songs we used to sing together . . .

What are some of the things that have helped you on your grief journey so far?

Think about it. . . . It might not be easy to identify what helps. It might be personal and private: lighting a candle, writing in your journal, or looking at photographs. It might be more public: getting together with family or talking with your friends. And it might be something you hadn't experienced before your loss: seeing a therapist or being part of a support group.

Just as everyone grieves differently, everyone heals differently too. Your grief will feel different a week, a month, and a year from now. It will continue to change as you live your life. You'll know more about it as time passes — what holiday triggers it, for example. And you'll know what helps — visiting the cemetery or deciding not to visit the cemetery. No one can tell you what will help, but I hope that the reflections below offer some ideas and outlets for your feelings.

But first, let me tell you for sure what *doesn't* help: doing things that are harmful to you and others. It may be tempting to try to numb your pain with drugs and alcohol, but I guarantee your pain will be worse for it. If you feel that your grief is leading you down a road that could be unhealthy for you, talk to someone you trust *right now* and ask for help.

Sometimes finding the things that do help takes a while — you have to go looking for them. And sometimes help is closer than you might imagine. It's there in a memory or in a song played loud or in a deep, slow breath.

> *What helps is knowing that I had all that time with him, and I feel I didn't waste it. I know that I was blessed to have known, loved, and be loved by him, and I feel sorry for the people who didn't and won't. He was a special person, and I think for that reason alone, he was taken away early. He was worth so much and was such a singularly wonderful person. It makes me appreciate him more than I might have if he hadn't died.* — Ella

> *Sometimes talking helps, sometimes writing helps, sometimes just breathing helps; it depends on the situation. Sometimes I like to play music really loud to block everything out, sometimes I'll raid the kitchen and eat everything in sight. It just depends on what kind of mood*

I'm in. Sometimes if your body tells you to do something, you should do it, as long as you are not hurting yourself or anyone else. — Hilary

Sometimes, help is all about just letting it out:

What helps is CRYING, talking to my dad about my mom before I was born. It is cool to hear stories about what she was like before I knew her, stuff I never got to ask her. She died before I was a full teenager, so I never really got to hear what her teenage years were like. . . . I was too young to really know to ask. — Matt

Crying helps so much — you just let it all out. Even if you're feeling down for no reason and feel like crying, DO IT. For me, running, jumping on the trampoline, and playing with my dog helps. Basically anything that requires a lot of energy. That way you have no energy to be upset. — Caitlin

Well, there are not many things that help me. One thing that helps quite a bit is writing and answering questions like this. It helps me to figure out what happened and how I am dealing with it. Another thing that helps is talking to other people. It can be anyone: adults, teens, little children,

151

*friends, anyone who will let you talk to them about your
loss. It also sometimes helps when someone just gives you
a hug, although it can also be annoying or uncalled for.
Something that helps, but I don't do it very often, is
crying. When you cry, it helps to just let everything out.*
— Beth

*Knowing that this is the worst it can get. I've survived
one of the worst, if not the worst, events of my life, and
I'm okay and a stronger person because of it.* — Casey

Writing, getting close to nature, looking at the stars, dancing.
— Suzanne

I have kept a journal since the hour I found out my dad died.
— Peter

People who feel compassion for you, but NOT pity.
— Katie

Several of the teens I interviewed responded that coming
to camp has helped. While I started the camp for exactly that
reason — to help kids who are grieving — I want to empha-
size that even if you can't come to camp, you can seek out
people who have been through what you have. Your school,

your doctor, your church, or a therapist in your area may be able to refer you to a support group or connect you with other grieving teens. Talking helps a lot, especially if you're talking to people who "get it."

Talking about your loved one with family and others who knew him or her can also be a big comfort:

What helps: exercise, Comfort Zone Camp, writing, talking to family (or talking to anyone in general), remembering times we shared, helping another person, seeing photos of her, being told I look or act like her, hearing songs we used to sing together, doing things we used to do (bake, paint, etc.), sunshine, spending time with her side of the family. — **Abbey H.**

One thing that helps is going to counseling. I don't like talking to people who nod their heads and say that everything is going to be okay. When I am angry about it, I just yell. I cry and scream. I have to relieve myself or I can't handle it, and I just want to pull out all of my hair. When I went to Comfort Zone Camp, my life was forever changed, and I always thought there was no one who felt like I did. That was a huge change, and it really helped. — **Melissa**

CZC, talking to anyone I trust, poetry, music, movies,
keeping active and open. — Jesse

My friends from camp who know exactly how I feel.
Listening to music that reminds me of my dad. Looking
at pictures and things that belonged to him. Writing in
my journal. — Lora

I wrote in Chapter 8 that finding people who knew your
loved one and are willing to share stories and memories can be
a huge help in keeping you connected to your loved one:

Telling or hearing stories about my dad. He and I were a
lot alike as far as our sense of humor is concerned, and it's
fun to hear about all the things that he did. Being able to
think about his life and laugh about the happy memories.
— Elizabeth

Knowing other teens who have experienced a loss has
been very helpful to me. I know that if I'm having a
hard time or missing my dad, I know I can call a
friend who will understand what I'm going through.
I can also be a support for my friends who have
experienced a loss, and I like to know that I'm
helping them. — Emily S.

*Looking through old photos and talking about my dad
helps. When I talk about him, it seems like he is still here.*

— Hannah

*I have a great extended family that helps support us. My
mom's parents are so good to us. They take lots of their
time to help us around the house, spend quality time with
my sister, and help my mom when she is really busy or
stressed. I know that God is teaching me a lot through
this experience. He has shown me how great my family is
and how precious life is. I've read several books on grief.
Some help, some don't. I think you really need to
understand it before you can write about it.*

— Emily L.

*I think what helps me the most is talking about my dad.
Every once in a while, I will just have some random
little thing to say about him. It helps me a lot to have
friends who don't mind me mentioning him every once
in a while.*

*It's also really great to spend time with my dad's
family. I love to learn more about him through his
brothers. They are always telling great stories
about him.*

— Mary

I like to look at pictures of my dad. That helps me a lot. I write a lot when I'm sad. It helps me to write everything I'm feeling. It also helps to look back and see how far I've come. I like to go to the cemetery every once in a while, just stay for a few minutes. I feel closer to him there. Sometimes I'll go down to the den in our house, which used to be his room, and just sit. I feel like he's there somewhere. I read all different kinds of books. They became like a safe haven for me after he passed away. Books helped me escape from reality for a while. Going to camp helps a lot. Talking to people who understand what I'm going through makes me feel a lot better. I like looking through his stuff once in a while. Sometimes I can smell him on stuff that is in his box. I like to sit and remember him, keeping the memories fresh in my mind, so I never lose them. — Cassie

A few things helped me "manage" or cope with the loss of my parents. I had a best friend who I told everything to. She was the one person who listened and knew everything I was dealing with. She was my rock.

Taking the risk of reaching out to people who somehow seemed like they "got it" also helped. There were a few guidance counselors, teachers, and coaches who went out of their way to take an interest in me or "check on" me. Did they fill that huge hole inside of me? No, not completely, but for a short time, they filled in a piece of the hole, which helped me get a little stronger.

"Letting it out" was crucial for me. I had so much *stuff* inside me, and a lot of it was deep pain. It helped me to keep a journal. I wrote in it all the time, anything from daily events to poems about my pain and loss. I also found myself writing letters and words of encouragement to myself. I realize now I was giving myself pep talks. And when I was done, I was kind of exhausted, but I always felt so much better.

Over time, I have found other things that help me to let it out. Things I know, wherever I am, are always with me, and they make me feel better. I can always find a piece of paper and start to write. I can still call my same best friend. I can always go for a walk or a run. I can always eat some chocolate. I can always do a crossword puzzle. I can always watch a silly old movie that makes me laugh. This is what works for me. It is different for everybody, but it's important to find those things that will work for you too.

11

GOOD THINGS THAT HAVE COME OUT OF LOSS

I'm lucky for what I have.

Loss changes us in many ways. The teens interviewed for this book have shared in previous chapters the ways in which they feel different from others because of their losses. However, those differences aren't always negative. Sometimes, the differences between yourself and others who don't "get it" are positive, and are a result of the good that has come out of your loss.

What are the good things that have come out of your loss?

At the time of her mom's death, Melissa had been in foster care:

> In my case, there are many good things that have come out of my loss. When my mom died, I moved to a new state. I started doing new things, and my interests started to expand. I love to horseback ride now and sing and dance. I plan to go to college. These are things I would never have been able to do if my mom was still alive. I am

determined now to make a difference, not only in my life, but in my community as well. I don't want to be another statistic. People are always saying, "Well, that girl's going to grow up to be just like her mother and do drugs and become an alcoholic." I will NEVER be a drunk or a smoker. I want to prove people wrong. I would fail as a person if I became like my mom.

I have come to understand that life is about going on and beyond. I want to reach the sky. I understand that you should always spend every moment you can with your family and let them know you care. Don't wait. Tell your family you love them. The loss of my mother also makes me want to make her proud of the daughter she left behind.

Peter was 12 when his father committed suicide. Three years later, he reflects on what he considers the "good" things that have come out of his loss:

My appreciation for what I have. I used to think I wanted it all. Now I'm content with what I have and don't care if someone else's is better. I'm lucky for what I have. I still have my mom and sister and a huge extended family. I could have nothing. Losing someone shows what you still have and what you can still lose.

Jesse was 12 when her father, who had been abusive, died. Now, five years later, her family's situation has changed for the better:

> I moved to a good area with a great stepdad and
> wonderful friends.

Here is what other teens have to say about "something good":

> I am glad to have the maturity that I do at my age.
> While it really hurt to lose my dad, I feel like I am
> better equipped to help others with hardships they may
> face in their lives. In my group of friends, I have often
> been referred to as the "group therapist," because my
> friends trust me enough to come to me with their
> problems. Also camp has been a blessing — does it ever
> get redundant? As I've said countless times to countless
> people, the most rewarding thing is to be able to give back
> what camp gave to me — to help kids with loss through
> their grief, based on what I learned from my own.
>
> — Elizabeth

> A few good things have come out of my loss. . . . I have
> been motivated to do well in school in honor of my father,

and I have upheld morals that he would be proud of. I also find it easier to talk to certain people, and when kids at my school experience a loss, I'm always there to listen to them or give them advice.   — Emily S.

I made new friends who are more like me, and I was made more aware of the real world.   — Hannah

I think that from every event or situation, there is good and there is bad. They are not in balance, necessarily, but it's a bit like yin and yang — a bad event can produce good things, just as a good event can produce bad things. I think in this case, this event has defined my life — I wouldn't be who I am today or will be in twenty years or fifty years if this hadn't happened. I wouldn't know the people I know, I wouldn't be in the same school, the same house, and who knows how many other variables. My life, while not based completely around this event, was nevertheless put on a path that can't go back and is the not same as if it hadn't happened.
                — Ella

I'm much closer to my mom and sister. I was very much a daddy's girl before he died, but now I've had the opportunity to be very close to both of my parents. Also

161

I got to go to camp. Comfort Zone has made such a huge impact on my life. I feel so different there than anywhere else. I'm completely comfortable talking about my loss, and I've found lots of people who love me very much and have had enormous impacts on my life. They inspire me. I've even decided that I want to work with camping organizations as a full-time career, due in large part to my experiences with Comfort Zone. I'm not glad that my dad died, but I am glad that it allowed me to find such a great community of support and comfort.

— Emily L.

I have become much closer with my aunt, cousins, and sister. My extended family has become a much more cherished part of my life. — Abby O.

My sense of responsibility. The idea that I can overcome daily trials and tribulations. Closer family ties (on my mother's side). Changing me as a person. — Abbey H.

My faith is stronger. I don't participate in risky behavior. I have made so many friends and met so many amazing kids, teens, and adults at camp, who I would have never met otherwise. — Lora

I have learned to cope with difficult situations that come up (most of the time), and I can often help my friends when they are hurting, because I can relate to them.

— Suzanne

My mother and I have become closer than ever. I changed schools, and now I have a lot of friends. I think I've become a stronger person mentally, and now I'm living life more fully.

— Hilary

I have met so many other great kids and adults who have helped me along the way. I have been given a chance to be a part of as great an organization as CZC, and I have been able to help little kids as a result of my loss. I have also become a stronger person, and I know that I can handle anything that happens in my life now.

— Casey

Well, a lot of times I think that my life is horrible and everything is going wrong and why did my dad have to die. But then I realize that I have learned so much from my father dying. I have learned to be more independent, become more mature for my age, and found a place that welcomes anyone, any loss, any age, or personality. This place is camp. I have learned about grief, found the

friendships that I will never abandon, and a place where
I feel that I won't be made fun of. Since my dad died, I
have changed in both good and bad ways. In some ways, if
my dad had not died, I would not have [experienced these
things].   — Beth

I have become a more motivated and outgoing person, trying
to live my life to the best possible standards. Even though I
have lost my mother, I know she would want me to be happy,
so I am really enjoying life every day through the good
and the bad. That is a gift I can thank my mom for.
                                                      — Matt

Sometimes the good that comes out of loss is growing closer
to people we never expected to, as Cassie has discovered:

I am a stronger person for having lived through such a
big loss. I've had experiences that have made me a better
person. I have become more sensitive to life. I am not
afraid to show emotion anymore. I have learned not to
take things for granted.

Something very good that came out of my loss was
becoming closer to my grandma. My grandma and I were
never close when I was younger, but my dad's death
brought us together. I learned that I could talk to her, and

she is always there for me when I need her. I have become very close to her, and I am so glad.

I learned who my true friends were. Some people couldn't be around me. They didn't know how to act, so they just ignored me. I found friends who stood by my side and helped me through all my ups and downs. One friend stayed with me every weekend, the whole month after my dad passed away. She came with me to Christmas shop that Christmas after he died. She encouraged me to go back to school, and she was there with me the day I went back, holding me up when I thought I couldn't handle it alone. I found friends who are still there for me now. They are there for me when I'm sad now and when I just miss him.

Another good thing that came out of my loss was my stepdad. It's hard for me to say that, because in a way I feel like it's betraying my dad. But he has been there for me. He's helped me when I needed it and stepped back when he knew I didn't want it. He loves my mom, and so that is a good thing that came from my loss. My dad wanted my mom to go on with her life and get married again. He told her that. So I know my dad would be happy.

Maybe you are at a completely different point and you can relate to what 14-year-old Eamon, whose dad died on 9/11, says:

I don't think anything good has come out of my loss.

If you feel this way, that's okay and honest. It is where you are on your journey. You just haven't traveled far enough down the road yet, but you will get there. There is good stuff that comes out of loss — it is sometimes slow to show itself, but it will happen for you too.

I'm many years into this journey and continue to discover good things that have come out of my loss. Starting Comfort Zone Camp was something good. And this book is something good, hopefully helping to make your journey easier than mine. Would I wish that journey on anyone else? No. Am I a better and nicer and more intuitive person from having experienced the death of my parents? Definitely. Am I stronger in most ways than I was before? Absolutely. I am now at the point (remember, *many* years into this) where wearing the label "Dead Parent Kid" is so much a part of who I am that the thought of having parents now is actually hard to imagine. I know I am a much better mom because I am aware that something could happen and my kids and I might not have each other nearly as long as we should. (Even though parenting seems a long way off, you will parent your kids differently as a result of your loss.)

This is just a small list, but it covers the key issues. Probably one of the best things that has come out of my loss — but took a while to really put into practice — is learning to have faith in something (like healing or risking loving new people), even when I can't see the end result. As you know so well, there are no "guarantees" in life — we can't look into a crystal ball and know our futures. But we *can* take our losses and the good and the bad things that have come out of them and live the best lives we can. Healing happens in different ways for different people; healing will happen for you.

12

LIVING WITH LOSS

You're not the only one!

Some of the most reassuring words of all are from other kids like you who are *living* with the loss of a parent. When I interviewed these teens, the first question I asked is what they'd want to tell other grieving teens if they were writing a book. Here's what they had to say (I think you'll see how I came up with the title for this book):

> *You're not the only one!*   — **Philip**

> *First of all, they are not alone. I know I've seen kids at my school lose family members, and many of them don't realize how many people there are at our school to relate to. Many of these teens are put at the center of attention at school because of their loss, and I think it would be helpful for them to realize there are people at school to talk to.*
>
> *Also I would want teens with a fresh loss to know that it gets better. At first things are terrible, and they will be for a while, but once the first year passes, so many*

people feel much better. And it's important for teens to know that feeling better and less sad is by all means okay. Being happy does not make your loss less but makes you a stronger person. — Emily S.

Grief doesn't go away. It will be with you for the rest of your life, and it's okay to be sad. Just because months or years have passed and outsiders think that you should be over it, that's not the case. You will never be completely over it, and that's okay. — Elizabeth

There are lots of other people out there who understand what you are going through. Don't be afraid to let them in. Those relationships can be some of the most important ties in your life. — Emily F.

Grieving the loss of a loved one is a lonely thing. Most importantly, I would tell other grieving kids that they are not alone! For a long time, I felt completely alone while I was trying to grieve for my dad's death. I never talked to anyone about him or anything, but after a little time, I found that I had a few friends who had also lost a parent, so I began to talk about my dad. And slowly I realized that I was not completely alone anymore.

— Mary

I would want to tell them that they are not alone in the world. Other people their age have experienced a loss. And I would tell them that it is okay to cry. Crying helps the bottled-up emotions release, and it feels GOOD! Lastly, I would tell them to be happy, because though this experience is painful, there is still so much to live for.

— Hannah

I would tell them that it's going to be okay. Someday the clouds will lift, and you'll see brighter skies. It may take a long time, but you have to keep on going. I would tell them that they are not alone. There are a lot of teens out there dealing with the same things. I remember feeling like I was the only one going through so much pain. I was the only one in my school who had lost a parent, so I was essentially alone. But in the grand scheme of things, you're not alone. Talk to someone; it helps so much. Talking about what you're feeling can get some of the weight lifted off your shoulders. Write. It doesn't matter what you write — it could be a story, a poem, lyrics, or in a journal — but write. It can make a world of difference.

— Cassie

Your loss is so very important. Don't feel as though it is insignificant or as though you are somehow less strong than other people. You are allowed to hurt as much as you want, for as long as you want, and your true friends will be with you for all of it. — Abby O.

I'd want to tell them that they're not alone and that it won't go away with time, but the sadness and loneliness will come in smaller segments, farther apart, eventually.

— Casey

It's okay; someday things are going to be all right again. And, hey — feel how you want — don't let anyone tell you how you should feel. It's your head, not theirs.

— Peter

Work hard so you can show your parent or someone you lost you won't give up, that you will do your best for them.

— Kimberly

One thing I would tell another teenager my age is that it is not your fault. Grief is an everlasting process. You can't just suddenly get over it. It will always be there. I want all grieving teenagers to know that it is okay to cry. If you don't cry and you keep it all inside, then one day everything is going to catch up with you, and there will be a flood of tears. Teenagers should know that they can get through it. That although it will be hard, you still have your entire life to live. — Melissa

Keep that person alive in yourself and your family. Talk about them with family, friends, and anyone else who will listen. Don't try to hold in your feelings. It feels so much better to let them out and share them with other people.

— Emily F.

Everyone says to give it time and things will go back to normal. Well, they don't. Time doesn't make it easier, it just makes it different. It's okay to feel your loss. It's okay to remember the good times too. Find people to confide in that you trust. Find ways to give your loved one's death meaning and know they are always with you.

— Lora

Keep cool as well as you can. Pain can be overwhelming, so just sit and think as well as you can about all the good things: They're in a better place, they're not hurting anymore, etc.

— Caitlin

I would tell them not to feel any guilt (especially if their loss was from suicide). I would also tell them to cry and

grieve. I tend to bottle things up inside, which is not good, and I know that, but still I continue to do it, and I would tell them to steer themselves away from doing that.

— Brittany

My book would never end. Every day, I learn something new about grief and living without a family member. I will tell you that life goes on. It is going to be easy at times, but other times it is going to be extremely hard.

— Beth

I would tell other grieving kids that healing takes time. The time period is different for everyone. You probably will never be fully healed, and you will NEVER forget what happened, no matter how hard you try. You can never change what has happened. It is not your fault; some things just happen, and you can't do anything to stop them. Talking to a grief counselor is a good way to deal with pain, and sometimes writing in a journal is good also. If you need help, TELL SOMEONE. You can't always deal with problems that large on your own.

— Hilary

Remember those lines I wrote about in the foreword — the one line for you on your grief journey, the one line for me walking beside you, and the other lines for the teens who shared their stories in this book? We are all here with you. When you need us, open this book and read our stories. When you're ready, share your story with someone you trust.

13

IF YOU COULD SAY ONE MORE THING . . .

I would say, "I love you."

What would you say to your loved one if you could say one more thing? The answer probably feels obvious — "I love you" is certainly at the top of the list for most people. And even though I asked teens about the "one" thing they'd say, almost everyone I interviewed wanted to say more.

Of course, we want to say more! It stinks that our loved ones aren't right by our sides to talk with. They were taken from us too early. We didn't have enough time to talk with them, grow up with them, and get to know them better. Your teen years are a time of so much growth and so many milestones, from school and sports to dating and driver's licenses. Our loved ones didn't have enough time to watch us grow and get to know us either.

Do you ever find yourself "talking" to your loved one, either silently or out loud? Telling him or her about a good grade or a bad date? Imagining his or her response? You're not crazy. This is normal, and for kids (and adults) who do this — it feels good. This is you speaking from your heart and trying to stay connected. Sometimes the things you have to say might guide you to good memories, as in Elizabeth's response about what she'd say to her dad:

> *I'd just reiterate over and over and over again how much I love him. And thank him for doing things that nobody else in my life does. He'd come home from work every once in a while with presents for all of us, just because. And if he was at home and had nothing to do, he'd find me wherever I was in the house and tell me he loved me, and that was it. And he'd tell me what a great singer I was, even if I wasn't singing. And he'd tell me how pretty I was, even if I was in my pajamas and had bed head. I'd tell him how much these things meant to me and how much I wish I could have caught them all on tape, so I could watch it over and over again and never, ever forget.*

Elizabeth's sister, Emily S., spoke directly to their dad when she responded:

> *I love you and miss you very much. I'm sorry for all the times we fought, and I wish you could be here to see me*

grow up. I'm doing my best to live my life the way you
would want me to.

When you lose a parent at a young age, you can't help but focus on things left "unsaid," as is the case for 17-year-old Cassie:

I really don't think I could just say one thing to my dad.
There are so many things that were left unsaid when he
passed away. I would tell him that he was the best dad in
the world and that 14 years were not enough with him. I
would tell him that I love him so much, and he is always in
my heart no matter where I go. I would tell him that I will
always keep all of our memories with me wherever I go in
life. And that everything I do, I do in memory of him.

Thinking of all the things left unsaid to your loved one is a huge weight to bear. It can lead to other powerful feelings, such as regret and guilt. People of all ages who suffer the loss of a loved one grieve over things left unsaid and undone.

But guilt is another can of worms I'd like to open right now: If you're feeling guilty because of some bad behavior that occurred before your parent died or even because, in anger, you might have wished them dead at times, you need to talk about those feelings as soon as you can. Why? Guilt can make your grief journey even more challenging. Cassie explains:

> For the first few years after my dad passed away, all I could feel was guilt. I blamed everything on myself. He died of a heart attack, and I thought that I made it happen. To me, it was natural to feel guilty. I just knew that I did something to cause it and that was it. It used to tear me up inside. I always had stomachaches and bad migraines because of all the guilt I felt. For a while, I believed with all my heart that I caused him to die. When people would say that it was just meant to happen and no one was to blame, I would think in my head, "No, you're wrong, I'm the one to blame." I used to run "what ifs" through my head constantly. Some of them were "What if I had been a better daughter?" "What if I hadn't fought with him?" "What if I had helped more around the house?" or "What if I had done something to save him?" I had a hard time concentrating in school because I was always thinking about it. It overtook my mind. I had everyone telling me that it was no one's fault, it just happened. But inside, I just kept on blaming myself. But as I got older, I began to think rationally, and I started to respond to all the "what ifs" that ran in my head. Slowly, I realized that it wasn't my

fault. I started to research the cause of his death and
learned that I couldn't have prevented it, and I couldn't
have saved him after he had the heart attack.

When I asked Cassie what she would say to another teen trying to overcome feelings of guilt, she responded:

I would tell them that they did not do anything wrong,
though it may seem like it. Especially for people who lost
a loved one suddenly, your mind begins to try and think
up things to justify what happened. But they have to
remember that nothing they did or didn't do could have
prevented their loved one from dying. Sometimes guilt just
takes time to wear away. When you are vulnerable, your
mind plays the blame game. But as time goes by and you
become stronger, you can overtake those guilty feelings.

Being sad about missed opportunities to tell your loved one how you feel about them is a natural and difficult part of the grief process. Still, I want to remind you that you're dealing with a totally unfair situation — we don't expect our parents to die when we're young. If you're feeling guilty about an argument or anything else that occurred right before your parent died, perhaps before you had a chance to talk about it, please talk *now* to someone about it. Start with your surviving parent — he or she may have reassuring insights about your loved one's feelings for you that will ease your mind.

There are times at camp when a teen expresses feelings of guilt associated with a sense of relief, especially in situations where there was unhealthy behavior. Healing Circle leader Kathy O'Keefe notes that if you were angry at your parent for being abusive or neglectful, you may find yourself torn between feeling relieved you don't have to deal with that anymore and grieving the things you miss about your parent — or the parent you wish you'd had. The one thing Melissa would tell her mom now focuses on how she wants to behave differently from the way her mother did during her life:

> *If there was one thing I could say to my mother, I think it would be, "Don't worry, Mom, I'm going to be stronger than you, and I will make you proud."*

In the case of a sudden or tragic loss, things get complicated because there are even more unanswered "whys." Take Peter and Brittany, who both lost their fathers to suicide:

> *I'd ask WHY? I know that depression made my dad think he was unwanted, but WHY? Why couldn't you have waited, just a little longer, for the medication to kick in?*
> — **Peter**

Why? We could have gotten help for you. Mom and I love
you so much, and I will always be your daddy's girl.
                                          — Brittany

Jesse's father died of cancer, but she also dealt with some
"whys" and has let go of some of the anger she had toward her
abusive dad:

I needn't judge you now, since you're in the presence of
the best judge in the universe.

If your relationship with your parent was troubled, then
you too need to talk to someone about your feelings. Try not
to judge yourself too harshly.

The question of what teens would want to say to their lost
loved ones raises something that many teens at CZC have
talked about and found comforting. Sixteen-year-old Hannah's
dad died when she was 9. Eighteen-year-old Lora's father died
when she was 10. Both find comfort in the idea that their dads
are "watching over" them:

I love you. Mom, Miles and I are doing great. We all miss
you very much. We still talk about you all the time. I

*wish with all my heart that you were still here to watch
me grow up. Somehow I know you are watching. There is
so much I want to tell you, but I think in some way you
already know what I am going to tell you.* — Hannah

*I love you, and I'm sorry we didn't have very much time
together, but I know you're always watching over me!*
— Lora

I asked Lora to talk more about what it feels like to her to
imagine her father "watching over" her:

*When I was a little girl, my dad once told me never to
stop dancing. As I went through middle and high school I
continued to dance, and the last few years of high school,
I joined a competitive dance group. I always felt like my
dad was watching me when I danced, because he had always
wanted me to keep dancing. I also felt like he was watching
me when I did things that he never got to see, like chorus
concerts and playing the piano. He died right before my
first chorus concert when I was in the fifth grade, and
ever since then, at chorus concerts, I felt like he was watching
me. I've also had times in which I knew the situation
was practically hopeless when I felt like he had a hand*

in making things work out. For instance, I applied for a scholarship from the army (my dad was a lieutenant colonel in the Army Reserves), and I didn't have enough information or the appropriate documentation for most of the application. Somehow I managed to get the scholarship anyway, and I really feel like my dad had a hand in it. It really keeps him alive inside me and makes me feel protected and safe when he's close in my memory.

In a sense, imagining you could say one more thing to your loved one is also an opportunity to say good-bye if you weren't able to do so, catch them up on what has been going on since they died, or just to reflect on your entire relationship with them. Saying "one more thing" is a way to tell them what they mean to you. At camp, we do an exercise I remember doing first in a grief support group: We write a letter to our loved ones. When I did this the first time some years ago, I thought it was really bizarre and abstract, and I put off writing my letter to my mom until the day it was due, because I just couldn't get into it. But when I finally sat down and wrote, it ended up being a really powerful and healing thing to do. After that, we wrote a letter back to ourselves from our loved ones. I thought I'd share part of these letters, which were written before I started Comfort Zone Camp:

Dear Mom:

If I had five minutes with you, what would I say to you? . . . I would say I am so sorry that you had to go away so early in my life. . . . I would want to know what was your greatest joy and your biggest regret. . . . I would want your image and memory and unconditional love to burn bright in me and be able to draw strength from it. I'd want you to be able to be there for me to help me when I struggle with difficult decisions and to help me to be able to make good decisions. Mom, this is so sad. I am so sorry your life wasn't easier with my father and that you had to miss out on seeing your children grow up and all that you missed as a result. . . .

And Mom replied . . .

I love you so much, and you need to remember I did not want to leave you. You were my pride and joy, and I am so proud of you now, as I always have been. You have been so strong and so brave. I have never left you, Lynne. I have always been with you. Every day, I see your successes and your failures . . . I know you feel like you are alone sometimes and that no one understands or is even aware of your pain. That is just not so. You are never alone. We are always with you. . . .

I know that you think you don't know me and that
you don't remember me well. Please remember these words:
You know more about me than you think you do. You are
my legacy. I live on through you. You have always been so
special, and you always will be. Use your gifts, your
talents, and knowledge as a tool for growth and as an
instrument to heal not only yourself, but to help others. . . .

To this day, I keep those letters to and from my mother in a special place, and I break them out and read them every now and then.

Regarding the feeling of being "watched over," it is usually a really good thing, and it helps us feel connected. I know of kids (and adults) who swear they have either seen their loved one sitting at the end of their bed, for example, or have physically felt their presence. I have experienced powerful dreams in which I can see my parents or talk to them and sometimes even ask them questions about death. I've also experienced what many people talk about: dreaming they never died and then waking up feeling it is so real that I can't shake the dream and just want to go back to sleep and reconnect with them. Again, these things are usually comforting but can also be disturbing or can just freak you out. It's all a perfectly normal part of grieving.

I hope reading this chapter has brought you closer to the

idea that "talking" to your loved one, saying the things left unsaid or just simply saying good-bye can be healing. I'll close with two very different responses, both of which I bet we can all relate to:

> *I would rather have a really big bear hug than say*
> *anything to Daddy.* — Emily F.

> *I love you and I miss you. And can you believe*
> *Steinbrenner lost Pettit?* — Hilary

14

Going Forward, Moving On

I will tell you that life goes on. . . .

What do the phrases "going forward" and "moving on" mean to you? Just like everything that has to do with loss, they are going to signify different things to different people.

> *"Moving on" is just one of those things that isn't in my sight. I just don't think that I can. It's like I can't see the end of it, so how do I "move on"?* — Peter

Part of healing is having faith in something, even when you can't see the end result. It's difficult, but it can be done. That faith can comprise a lot of things — faith in God, yourself, a brighter future, or even faith in knowing that the worst that can happen to you is over.

I believe the worst that can happen to me in my life has already happened. I believed that as a kid, and I believe it today. My tomorrows represent the promise of better and happier days, so I want to stick around and enjoy all the good stuff that has yet to come. I also believe I can handle anything that comes my way — again — because I know it will *not* be the worst thing that has ever happened to me. So I can get through it.

"Moving on" means traveling away from the loss, which also means traveling farther away from the experiences with your loved one and filling the space with new experiences and new people who often have no connection to the person you lost. I met my best friend, Nancy, in the seventh grade. My dad died the day before seventh grade started. She has now been my best friend for 29 years (yikes!), and she never knew either of my parents. Moving on can also be sad or bittersweet. We know we are healing, but we are letting our lost parent go in one sense and finding it harder to maintain the connection. Here's how Emily S. sums it up several years after losing her dad:

> *In the beginning, it was really hard to accept the reality that he was never coming home again. Now the hardest thing is the fact that I can't remember my dad. His voice, his smell, and even his face are all leaving my memory. I have pictures, but there are only a few and none of them captures him as a person. I've also felt really bad lately because I feel like I sometimes forget about my loss. I know it sounds terrible, but I often go for days without thinking about my dad, and it makes me feel awful.*

There can be guilt from moving on and guilt from feeling good or allowing yourself to laugh and have fun again. Somehow it seems disloyal. Some kids and adults don't want to let go of the pain, because they are afraid that means they are letting go of the connections too. You will move forward, and your pain will become hazier. I'm not saying you'll completely let go of the loss — certain things will always be embedded in your mind: the death and the funeral, for example. But if you work to keep connected to your loved one, find the good that comes with your loss, and focus on what helps, you will lead a happy life despite your loss.

Surviving this loss is a choice. You can choose to be a survivor or a victim. I chose and I still choose to survive. Don't let your loss beat you.

Melissa and Abbey H. have been where you are and have this to say:

> *At one point I wanted to give up too. I wanted to leave*
> *this world. Then I realized that I couldn't do that because*
> *then I would turn out to be just like my mom. You need*
> *to know you can get through it. Although it will be hard,*
> *you will have your entire life to live.*   — Melissa

> *Initially it stinks, but you will be able to pick yourself*
> *back up and start living again. It is really hard at first,*

but eventually (at least in my case), you realize they would want you to have a happy life. — Abbey H.

Melissa and Abbey H. made the choice to **SURVIVE.**

You have finished this book and finished one marathon. Keep going on your grief journey. Think about what runners do to train for a marathon: They condition themselves. They nourish themselves with things that are good for them. They pace themselves. They get people to run with them. They don't do it alone. They keep working to increase their endurance and push themselves a little farther every day, far past what they ever thought was humanly possible. Once they start the race, they notice people along the way who are standing on the sidelines cheering for them.

You can cross that finish line!!!! It will be your greatest personal accomplishment. I am on the sidelines cheering for you.

About Comfort Zone Camp

Comfort Zone Camp is the nation's largest nonprofit bereavement camp for children. Founded by Lynne Hughes and her husband, Kelly, the camp serves kids ages 7 to 17 who have lost a parent, sibling, or close loved one, all at no cost. Since 1998, the camp has helped guide more than 1,800 children through their grief, providing a safe, nurturing environment, where kids can have traditional camp fun while at the same acquire tools to help them cope with their losses. Staffed by trained volunteer counselors, including many grief professionals, Comfort Zone Camp offers camp sessions throughout the year.

Camps typically serve thirty-five to forty children, each of whom is paired with a volunteer "big buddy." Activities include games, arts and crafts, and small Healing Circles^{SM} led by grief counselors. A memorial service, attended by campers' family, is held at the conclusion of each camp. Children are allowed to return subsequent summers. Special camps just for teenagers are also available.

Most camps are held in the Richmond, Virginia, area,

attracting campers from all over the United States. Since the tragic events of September 11, 2001, Comfort Zone Camp has held satellite camps in the New York metropolitan area for 9/11 victims' children. Those camps are now open to any grieving child. Comfort Zone Camp anticipates establishing a permanent camp facility in central Virginia, which will be the first of its kind in the nation.

Please visit **www.comfortzonecamp.org** to learn more about Comfort Zone Camp.